Dream Palaces
Going to the pictures in Southampton

Written, compiled and edited by
Bill White
Sheila Jemima and Donald Hyslop

Photography
by
John Lawrence

Transcription - Janet Hall-Patch

Editorial assistance and additional research - A. G. K. Leonard

Any profits made from this publication
will go towards future projects
covering the people's history of Southampton.

Published by Southampton City Council

Produced by Oral History Unit, City Heritage Services
Civic Centre, Southampton SO14 7LP
The Oral History Service is provided by City Culture.

CONTENTS

Going to the Pictures 1

Early Years of Films in Southampton 4

Theatres, Music Halls, etc. 11

Standard .... "Cowboys, Tom Mix, Rudy Valentino and no talkies" 15

Picture Palace .... "A penny each to go to the pictures" 17

Kings .... "It was like walking into a big cavern" 19

Carlton .... "The cosiest picture hall in Southampton" 21

Imperial 22

Gaiety .... "A bit like a Turkish Mosque" 23

Picture House .... "Patronised by Royalty?" 25

Clock Tower .... "Living in another world for a few hours" 27

Empire/Gaumont/Mayflower ..... "The local people would get on stage and give a show" 28

Regal/Odeon .... "Ginger the cinema cat" 30

Forum .... "Snogging in the back row" 34

Classic .... "Free milk shakes in the café" 37

Neighbourhood Cinemas 39

Picturedrome/Queens/Roxy ..... "Look who's behind you!" 40

Plaza .... "The illuminated Compton Organ" 42

Scala/Lyric .... "Frankenstein, Dracula and the Mummy!" 46

Palladium .... "Flicker-free projection" 47

Broadway .... "They were stars then" 50

Plaza Hall, Portswood Road 51

Savoy .... "I suppose you called it courting" 52

Shirley Electric .... "Jessie Balderson the Musical Director" 53

Atherley .... "The best tuppence worth in the world" 55

Regent .... "The Shirley Bully" 59

Rialto .... "Part and parcel of cinema" 62

Bitterne .... "Great fun for the kids" 64

Ritz	*"The building seemed to lift up and come down again"*	65
Woolston	*"Left in mid-air with the train going over the cliff!"*	67
Other cinemas in the locality	*"The air raid warning has sounded"*	70
On the Liners	*"Watching the film backwards"*	72
Cinemas During World War Two	*"We never close"*	74
Post War Developments		80
Cannon/MGM	*"Everything light and bright"*	81
Harbour Lights	*"A new kind of cinema"*	83
Gantry	*"Popular, cult, foreign and arthouse"*	85
Ken Russell Interview		86
Indian Films	*"Used to take food with us, crisps or drink"*	87
Film Societies and Other Venues	*"Average bunch of bourgeoisie"*	89
Film Festival	*"A decade of success in the cinema"*	91
Interviewees		92
Acknowledgements		97
Bibliography		98

© Southampton City Council 1996

All rights reserved. No part of this publication may be reproduced, stored in a retrieval system or transmitted, in any form or by any means, electronic, mechanical, photocopying, recording or otherwise, without prior permission in writing from Southampton City Council.

ISBN 1 872649 06 6

First Published 1996

Design by Graphics Services,
printed by Printing Services, Southampton City Council.

FOREWORD
by Councillor Eddie Read, Chair of the Leisure Services Committee

'There can't be many people who have not had a lasting impression or memory from visiting the cinema. I am no different; I could write a whole chapter on my experiences of 'the pictures' (as I still prefer to call them), some of which I'm sure wouldn't get past the Editor, so I'll tell you just one or two.

Woolston cinema took up Saturday mornings for nearly all my early childhood and created for me a life long love of film. My first adult film was the *African Queen* which I saw by mistake. I had coaxed my mother to take me to see a Roy Rogers film - yes, I admit to Roy being my first hero. Unfortunately I had got the date wrong and at first I was disappointed, but soon got absorbed in that truly wonderful film. Another memory that comes back to me is that of school holidays when there was a film on that my mates and me wanted to see and, of course, as usual we were stony broke. What we used to do was to raid our parents and relatives for empty beer bottles, take them back to the pubs and off-licences, collect the refunds and have a great day out at the flicks. Then there was the time my brother and cousins were all taken to the cinema on the day of my grandmother's funeral. Oh, but that's a long story...

I am sure that, like me, this book will evoke your own memories, and I hope you get many hours of pleasure when reading it. My own personal thanks to everybody who contributed - you have really proved the important role the cinema has played in all our lives and what is a vital part of Southampton's history.

Happy film going.'

EDITORS' INTRODUCTION

Visits to the cinema have always featured prominently in the memories of so many local people whose life stories have been recorded for Southampton City Council's oral history unit. The idea for the book came about during the 1991 Southampton Film Festival when City Heritage Services organised a bus tour visiting the sites of the various Southampton cinemas. Our guide was local historian Bill White and during the event it became evident that over the years he had amassed a wide knowledge of the subject from the dates of openings and closing through to anecdotes of staff and cinema cats! The tour was repeated the following year, this time augmented by tape recordings from the oral history archive of Cinemagoers experiences played over the bus audio system. From these beginnings then came the idea to produce a book combining Bill's knowledge and the first hand accounts of those who worked in or visited Southampton cinemas.

The material contained within this book comes from a variety of sources. Twenty seven people were specifically interviewed for this book, mainly those who have worked in the local cinema industry. Other first-hand accounts are taken from some of the 800 interviews which have been carried out for the oral history archive since 1983. In most cases quotes are attributed to interviewees but in some cases remain anonymous. The quotes have been selected in order to reflect a wide range of experiences of working in and visiting cinema in Southampton. Sadly some of the people featured have died since they were interviewed, but their tape recorded life stories will continue to be a valuable historical resource for future generations.

The photographs have been drawn from a number of local collections. We are indebted to the Southern Daily Echo, Braziers Builders, Southampton Archives Service, Ocean Pictures, Bitterne Local History Society, Sealink Stena and the many private collectors who have allowed us to reproduce photographs.

Photographs which have no credit come from the City Heritage Services Collections.

At the end of the book we have attempted to acknowledge all those who have helped us bring this book to fruition. If we have omitted anyone we apologise for the oversight.

In this centenary year of cinema this book celebrates one of the major leisure activities of this century which has brought pleasure to millions.

As Bert Mayell eloquently reflects:

"True cinema starts as a child, its your first cinema; now the first one I worked in was the Rialto but the first one I remember going in was Woolston and to me Woolston is the home of cinema, that's where all my dreams were nurtured; I've met the outside world through the front two rows in Woolston, fivepence a go and I wouldn't have changed it."

Sheila Jemima, Donald Hyslop. May 1996.

Dream Palaces

GOING TO THE PICTURES

Going to the pictures has been an important part of many people's lives for most of this century. Visits to the cinema feature strongly in millions of memories of childhood, growing up and courting days - although less so now than formerly; the "golden age" of the cinema spanned little more than fifty years, from around 1910 to the 1960's. Television and videotape have since brought films very much more into the home, changing the pattern of the public entertainment industry which at its peak in the mid/late 1940's attracted weekly audiences of over 30 million to Britain's cinemas.

The new popular art form was first introduced to a paying audience in a Paris café basement on 28th December 1895, when the brothers Louis and Auguste Lumiére used their Cinématographe machine to project moving pictures from film on to a sizeable screen.

Their invention was outstandingly effective among many developments in visual effects and projected images giving the impression of movement. These had long exercised a challenging fascination, embracing shadow plays (of great antiquity in the East and popular in Europe from the 18th century); panorama paintings illuminated as they were unwound; various optical toys and peep-show devices and magic lanterns, which over several centuries had become increasingly sophisticated machines, capable, with powerful lighting, of long distance projection in a large hall.

The inventors of cinema motion pictures combined this tradition and technology with the latest in photography, using continuous roll film, as marketed by the Eastman Kodak Company from 1888.

Their pioneering films quickly aroused appreciative interest in Britain, where public showings began in February 1896, soon extending from London to many other places. The first in Hampshire was at the Victoria Hall, Portsmouth, in August 1896.

Early film makers in Southampton. Exact location unknown.

DREAM PALACES

Southampton may have had a demonstration that year but the earliest showing recorded here seems to be the film of Queen Victoria's Diamond Jubilee procession, screened at the Philharmonic Hall, Above Bar, in December 1897.

Early film loops usually ran for only a minute or two and appealed primarily as novelties. At first, almost any scene or action served for films made quickly and cheaply - the arrival of a train, a street scene, a 'stop thief' chase, men playing cards; anything demonstrating movement. These were complemented by forerunners of the news reel, travelogue and natural history documentary, along with artistic, magic, comic and fantasy themes produced by ingenious photograph arrangements. An early example of local news film, dating from 1898, featuring a horse omnibus passing through the Bargate and Generals leaving for the Boer War, is held at the National Film Archive.

Such films were shown flickeringly in fairground booths; professionally as part of music hall and theatre programmes; and by individual enterprise in all sorts of halls, clubs and improvised premises. Audience demand for more sophisticated entertainment soon prompted the creation of fictional dramas - highlighted by *The Great Train Robbery* (1903) and the development of production and distribution networks offering films of steadily increasing length and story-telling artistry to exhibitors, on a regular rental basis.

That silent films were relatively cheap to make helped the profitable marketing of the output of European and American as well as British studios. By 1908 the supply was sufficient for cinemas to operate continuously for several hours a day, providing varied programmes changed twice a week, often with another different one on Sunday evening.

Their entertainment was essentially "popular"; seats ranged from 3d. to a shilling (5p) - at a time when many workers earned under £2 a week. As audiences grew, so did the competition between cinemas, which offered longer programmes in more comfort, even splendour, but still as cheap family entertainment.

In 1914 Italian versions of *Quo Vadis* and *Last Days of Pompeii* were screened in Southampton. Each was a three-reel feature, supported by a two-reel slapstick comedy, two single reelers, a Pathé Gazette and an episode of a serial like *The Operator at Lone Point*. Music to enhance and compliment the film stories and scenes was then provided by a combination of piano, violin and harmonium.

Some cinemas boasted a larger orchestra; even the smallest employed a regular pianist. By 1930 the advent of "talkies" had ended such accompaniments but a new form of musical entertainment during intermissions was offered by the distinctively toned cinema organ. Many will recall these mighty Wurlitzers rising into view, bathed in multi-coloured lighting.

The 1930's saw the building of a new range of luxury cinemas geared to top quality presentation of sound films to large audiences. All the older cinemas needed to install new sound systems; some, being smaller, found the changeover uneconomic and were unable to compete.

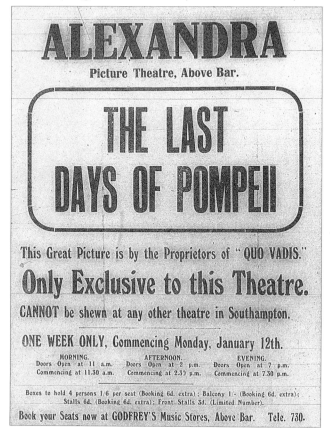

Advertisement of January 1914 from "What's On" for the Alexandra Picture Theatre.

Most of the pre-1914 first generation of cinemas had not been purpose-built but resulted from conversion of pre-existing theatres, music halls, other halls and premises including redundant chapels and skating rinks - roller skating had enjoyed great but short lived popularity in Edwardian times. An example of such changes of use was the Hampton at Hythe, serving as dance hall, roller skating rink and cinema.

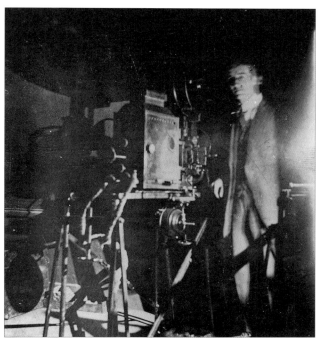

Early style projection room, probably at the Kings. Mr. Mansbridge at the machine. Corbishley Collection.

The proliferation of cinemas in the later 1900's was brought under specific licensing and building controls by the 1909 Cinematograph Act. Coming into effect on the first day of 1910, this made cinemas subject to annual licensing by local Councils, which ensured that they met fire and safety requirements e.g. no overcrowding, unobstructed exits with doors opening outwards and fire-resisting projection boxes, completely isolated from the auditorium; early films were highly flammable.

These controls provided a secure framework for the development of the cinema industry by responsible operators and promoted the construction of purpose-designed cinemas, with which Southampton was so well provided during the inter war years... as many older folk still vividly recall.

EARLY YEARS OF FILMS IN SOUTHAMPTON

Moving pictures were first shown in Southampton at the Philharmonic Hall in Above Bar, from 1897. The first venue for regular cinema programmes was the Empire Theatre in French Street, which in 1908 changed over from music hall to "animated photography" - presented twice nightly, with a different programme on Sunday evening and a Saturday afternoon children's matinee. This pattern was soon to be followed by a growing number of other "picture palaces".

Advertisement of January 1910 from "What's On" for the Philharmonic Hall. Seats could be booked at Mr H. P. Hodges' Music Saloon. Just over two years later Mr Hodges was to be a victim of the Titanic disaster.

The histories of the Philharmonic Hall and the Empire illustrate how films supplemented or superseded older forms of "live" entertainment.

The Philharmonic Hall was an impressive Victorian building, "an elegant and commodious hall erected at enormous expense", where the "grand inaugural concert" took place on 4th July 1865. The hall was leased for various forms of entertainment, which from 1897 onwards increasingly included "cinematograph exhibitions".

Initially these were often of the newsreel type, beginning with Queen Victoria's Diamond Jubilee procession and followed in 1898 by the Corbett v Fitzsimmons boxing match, advertised with some exaggeration as "two miles of life-size photographs", England v Australia cricket, the University Boat Race etc. Later films showed aspects of the war in South Africa, the Russo-Japanese War and events of more local topicality, such as highlights of several Southampton football matches at the Dell in 1908.

By then, dramas dominated the screenings and fiction films were the mainstay of the "colossal and most expensive programmes" offered by A. and H. Andrews' "World Renowned Pictures and Famous Orchestra". A notable feature in January 1909 was "that superb dramatic production *The Devil*, an out of the ordinary subject with a very healthy moral".

Later in 1909 the "Phil" was taken by the Walturdaw Co. Ltd., of London, the film distributors who already controlled the Empire.

They increased showings from once to twice nightly, with programmes changed twice weekly (the company had over 500 pictures available) and adopted "popular prices" of 3d., 4d., 6d., and 9d. Manager Fred Boustead promoted "refined and beautiful entertainment, constantly changing" in a hall "warmed throughout, the most comfortable entertainment house in Southampton" - to the extent that the "good old Phil" became the object of a take-over by another company with more ambitious plans.

EARLY YEARS OF FILMS IN SOUTHAMPTON

A pre-1914 postcard picture of Above Bar, showing the Alexandra Picture Theatre. To the right is a sign advertising the Hippodrome in Ogle Road.

These involved closing the hall for three weeks while it was "entirely reconstructed, redecorated and re-seated in the most modern and luxurious manner". Re-opened on 23rd October 1911 as the Alexandra Picture Theatre, it offered over 1,000 "roomy plush tip-up seats with arms" for continuous performances from 5 to 11 p.m., at prices still 3d. and 6d. for the stalls but raised to 1s. for balcony and 1s. 6d. each for the newly created boxes; seats were bookable in advance.

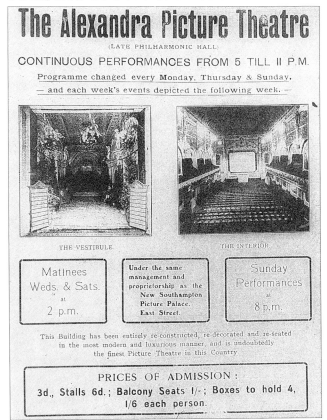

Advertisement of 1911 from "What's On" for The Alexandra Picture Theatre.

It was then claimed as "undoubtedly the finest Picture Theatre in this Country" and evidently received good patronage, for by 1914 it was providing continuous performances daily from 2.15 to 10.45 p.m. of programmes usually comprising five or six films - two or three dramas and two or three comics, plus news and other short items, all with "delightful appropriate music" under the baton of an ex-army bandmaster.

Publicity event at The Alexandra for Taming of the Shrew c1929. Southern Daily Echo.

A highlight of May 1914 was a week's showing of "Edison's Talking Pictures", billed as "The Eighth Wonder of the World"; in effect, players mimed to a gramophone record, the sound was not synchronised integrally with the film.

This "superior picture house" was outranked by new ones in the 1920's and closed in 1933 to be demolished to clear part of the site for the building of the Regal. Opened in 1934 (see later) and renamed the Odeon in 1945, this finally closed in 1993, to give way to commercial redevelopment of the site which by then had been identified with public entertainment for over a century and a quarter.

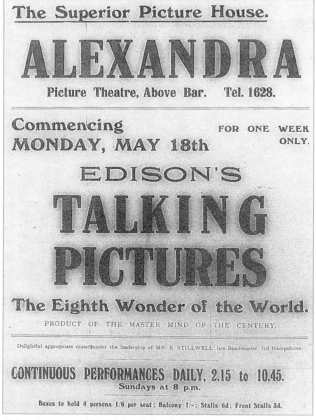

Advertisement of 1914 for Edison's Talking Pictures at The Alexandra.

Southampton's other pioneer cinema also had an interesting history. The Empire Theatre, between French Street and Bugle Street, was associated with the second Theatre Royal built in 1803 and the adjoining Rainbow Tavern, which from the 1850's operated as a music hall, under a variety of names. Burnt down in 1884 and rebuilt in 1886, it then became known as the Empire Palace Theatre of Variety.

In November 1908 it became a cinema, styled simply the Empire Theatre, offering programmes of "Walturdaw's Animated Pictures... absolutely the finest series in Southampton" - embracing farce, comedy, drama and travel. "Popular Prices" were 2d., 3d., 4d., and 6d., for showings at 7.00 and 9.00 p.m., along with a "Grand Children's Matinee" at 3.00 p.m. on Saturday (half price) and a "Biograph Concert" on Sundays at 8.00 p.m. - "special programme distinct from that of the week".

Unlike the more expensive and fashionable Philharmonic Hall/Alexandra, the Empire seems to have found little need for press advertising. Presumably locally displayed posters were sufficient for what must have been essentially a neighbourhood cinema - although it was by no means small, if the figure of 1,200 seats noted in 1915 was correct, and could originally claim to be the "Premier Picture Theatre" offering a "perfect picture, comfortable seats, warm and well ventilated".

One memorable film shown at the Empire was *Buffalo Bill's Wild West*, which ran for three days from 21st January 1914. Some patrons may have remembered William Cody's visit and the performance on the Marlands a decade earlier.

As cinema competition intensified in the 1920's the old Empire evidently found it harder to maintain its position. It was eventually obliged to close in 1925 and the building was afterwards demolished.

The Empire Palace Theatre, Bugle Street entrance. Pre 1908. Standing outside is Fred Mason who had taken over running the Empire after working at the Palace Theatre. It is reputed that when he left The Palace he was given a purse of gold. Corbishley Collection.

"The Alexandra, that was a converted hall. I think it was known first as a Philharmonic Hall and originally they used to show panoramic pictures there, you know on photographs or something, or paintings on a screen that used to be wound across."
O.H.A.

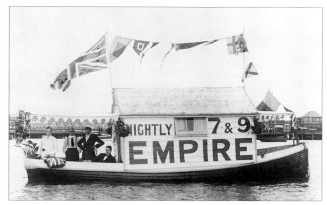

Empire house boat with flags and floral decoration brings a novel approach to advertising on Southampton Water. Corbishley Collection.

"When we were children we went to see a cowboy film, 'Buffalo Bill' I think it was. Well when we came out after the film was over we were given a black metal toy pistol in a thin brown leather holster. That was during the First World War. All the children got one."
Charles Grover

"There was a cinema in French Street and there was a projection box made of iron on the top, corrugated iron on the roof, and Archie Reade was up there and he used to wind the handle for the Pathé number one projector, you had to wind the handle at 75 revs a minute to keep the film going, silent, it was. He was always hanging around cinemas. He did a spell at Woolston Cinema and they had a fire there, the celluloid film caught fire but Archie got buckets of sand and water and they put up big No Smoking signs then, but all the cinemas banned smoking because of the celluloid film, very dangerous; he'd had lots of machines and he had one out of the Empire, a big portable sized machine in his little kitchen, shining through into the kitchen proper, out of the outhouse into the kitchen on a screen he nailed on the wall and he'd show us film on there, proper 35 mm films. He'd go to Wardour Street and pay £10 for a film, go to London for films. When we had the kiddies tea parties he'd come and bring his projector... and show a film for the kids indoors."
Thomas Hiett

EARLY YEARS OF FILM IN SOUTHAMPTON

Meanwhile, around 1908 there had been other smaller scale cinema ventures, in improvised premises not then subject to any licensing inspection and control.

Horace Williams' American Bioscope opened about 1908/09 in Adelaide Road, St. Denys in two empty shops. The Bioscope lasted a couple of years. There is a story that the owner built a shed at the back to install the projector and knocked a hole through the wall to project on to a screen. A patron remembers the piano being played by a teenage girl from Priory Road whose father played on the boats. Admission was a ha'penny and the

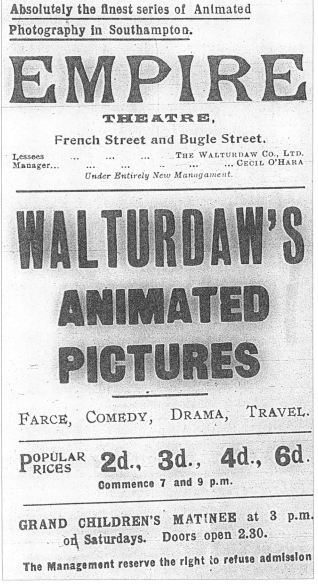

Advertisement of February 1911 from "What's On" for the Empire Theatre.

DREAM PALACES

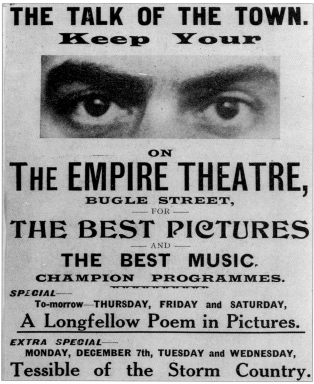
Empire advertising poster. Corbishley Collection.

commissionaire was Mr. Phillips, a retired policeman nicknamed "cock robin" because of his colourful uniform. The building later became Miss Peter's Dance Hall and now the much altered building is a small block of flats.

"The first film I ever went to was in Adelaide Road, in St. Denys and it was in a hall, just forms across, and I can see it now, I was scared stiff because the film was of big white horses and they were coming off the film and it seemed as though they were coming at you, oh dear, I was scared stiff. That was the first time I ever saw a movie film and it was just like rain all running down the film, horrible, but we thought it was marvellous."
Joyce Hare

The Cinematograph Act coming into force on 1st January 1910 put an end to such small cinemas, most of which vanished without trace. In Southampton, apart from the managers of the well established places of entertainment in the town centre, the only other application put before the Works Committee of the Borough Council in January 1910 was from William Mitchell of 145 Adelaide Road. Approval was made conditional upon his carrying out specific alterations to the premises to the satisfaction of the Borough Engineer; he seems not to have pursued the matter further.

In August 1912 Phillip Anderson's application for a licence in respect of the "Adelaide Picture Hall", St. Denys, was bluntly refused by the local authority.

Private Enterprise

It was, of course, still possible for enterprising individuals to set up semi-private little cinemas in their own houses and sheds, to cater informally for family, friends and neighbours, making some modest profit from the entertainment thus provided. One well known figure in Southampton in the early part of this century was Archie Reade.

"Archie Reade, he was born about 1900 in Southampton and he lost his leg in 1906 or 1908. There was a light gauge railway coming from the Empress Dock in the old docks taking the spoil round via Western Esplanade and dumping it by the Central Station, the power station; he was playing around on the line and an engine and fourteen trucks went over his legs. They took him in a wheelbarrow to the South Hants Hospital and sewed him up and he was there about three weeks and then sent home. He got £100 compensation which was regarded as quite good at the time. He had a pair of crutches when he came out of hospital and he smashed one because he couldn't get on with them and he used (only) one after that, and he used to get around quite good. He had a special boot with toes in and his father looked after him and then he was all round Canal Walk and earned a penny where he could because there was no proper jobs for disabled people in those days and he used to help the sweetmakers at the sweet shop at Canal Walk and he used to play football in goal, I don't know how he did that, but he did it! There was somebody in Canal Walk, a butcher, he had a bicycle outside and Archie saw this bike, he was looking at it and the chap said to him, if you can ride that bike to Eastleigh and back you can have it. So he gave him tuppence for the phone, Archie cycled to Eastleigh and he phoned up to say he'd got there and when he got back they gave him the bike. After that he went everywhere on the bike. He altered the bike by taking the crown wheels off, the pedal off on his bad side and he used to make his own crutch out of a shunter's pole and he made brackets to fix it on the bike and

he used to leap on over the back wheel... put one foot on the spindle and then leap forward onto the bike which he could do without falling off, but he had to have a fixed wheel cos he couldn't free-wheel with his leg being gone and he cycled everywhere like that. The only thing that beat him was when it was cold and frosty; if it was frosty he was finished, cos he'd fall off. He went all round, all over the place and everywhere on this bike."
Thomas Hiett

"Archie Reade's house, 1 Bell Street. He had one leg and no toes on the other leg. He was a coppersmith by trade and could make model steam engines. He had a cinematograph (mechanical) in his copper-house (back wash-house) and all the kids used to pay a penny to see a silent movie. Archie Reade turned a handle and the kids watched the film. About six kids at a time. It must have been in 1915."
Carlo Donnarumma

Enthusiastic amateurs like young Walter Olive, born in 1916, worked hard to save up enough to buy a projector so that he could put on film shows for his friends.

"I was known in those days as a boot repairer's runner and a man by the name of Mr. Hood had a boot repair business in Grove Street just above me and I used to get up at seven o'clock in the morning and carry a gigantic bag of repair boots, bigger than myself the bag was and take them off to Cleveland's just Below Bar in the High Street; that was in those days one of the top boot shops in the town, Cleveland's. I used to take this big bag of boots up there first thing in the morning, leave them outside and come back with another one, take them down to old Hood's and then during the morning he'd write out a list and when I came out of school I would go straight to Hoods get the order and go to East Street, Thomas the leather merchants in East Street, and get this order which usually consisted of a ruddy great big band of leather, which there again was bigger than myself in those days, and all the bits and pieces which I'd carry back to Hood and go indoors and have something to eat, whatever there was for dinner and go back to school and then repeat the same in the afternoon... ...I'd only be about twelve, if that, and I used to do this five days a week for a shilling, which was good money in those days, a

Oddfellows matinee at the Empire, Samuel Corbishley, who worked in many Southampton theatres and cinemas is on the right, standing beneath the exit sign. *Corbishley Collection.*

Archie Reade, cinema projectionist and film enthusiast. Private Collection.

treasure to us kids, so what we used to do, we used to go up, 'got any rubbish Charlie'... help yourself...

... so we'd fill up these sacks with rubbish, take them down in the garden and sort through them for a broken soldier or broken toy or something, this was real rubbish, treasure to us you see ...how we built the shed was we used to buy these cases off of Charlie and Grandad and I and Dad used to break these cases up, we built our own shed and in Granny Hyde's shop in Grove Street which was a little provisions store, she used to sell loose corned beef cut off. We used to get these seven pound tins and Grandad, being a tinsmith and a very good man at that, he would open up these tins and flatten them out and we covered the whole of the shed with corned beef tins and then on top of that we used to go down to the gas company and get a bucket of tar, which would be about thruppence, tar the top of the shed which was covered in tin, put newspapers on the top, a layer of newspaper and a layer of tar, making our own, what is commonly known now as roofing felt, and the shed was absolutely watertight, it went all over the shed, you see. Well, that was our shed."

Walter Olive

shilling. That was for the week, I used to give 6d. to Mum and have 6d. for myself and out of that I saved up enough money to buy a cinematograph in Samway's in St. Mark's Road and we used to give cinema shows in the shed at the bottom of the garden.... for marbles, cigarette cards, or whatever there was going...

...Oh we could get a dozen without any hassle...just a little hand projector, which the films in those days were continual roll films and you just whacked them on and you lit the lamp up inside...and you focused it on the screen on the shed wall and then turned the handle, 'come and see Ollie's cinematograph show'...

...We built, Grandad, Dad and I built the shed ourselves. We used to go and get the big packing cases from Woolworth's which he used to cut up and chop up and sell as bundles of firewood and in these big packing cases were stacks of rubbish and in the stacks of rubbish was little bits and pieces which was

Walter Olive outside Ascupart School. 1936. Private collection.

THEATRES, MUSIC HALLS, etc.,

From the early 1900's films were shown from time to time at Southampton theatres and music halls, normally supplementing but occasionally replacing the usual live entertainments.

Palace Theatre, Above Bar. Corbishley Collection.

The Palace Theatre (music hall) in Above Bar included early films in its Sunday evening concerts. From January 1909 "owing to the increasing popularity of Animated Pictures", more time was given to them in what were then styled "Bioscope and Band" entertainments at the "Popular Place for Perfect Pictorial Personation". That October it offered "the first and exclusive appearance in Southampton of the genuine Polar Expedition animated pictures" - for which four matinee showings were arranged. In 1910 "Tea and Pictures" sessions were introduced - 4.00 to 5.30 p.m., prices 3d. and 6d.

The Interior of the Palace Theatre c.1910, with the resident orchestra in front. Corbishley Collection.

While films continued on the Palace programmes, principally on Sunday evenings, they were also shown occasionally at the Hippodrome in Ogle Road (which operated as a variety house from 1905 until closing in 1939) and at the Grand Theatre.

Actors in a patriotic production pose for a photograph on the Palace stage. Corbishley Collection.

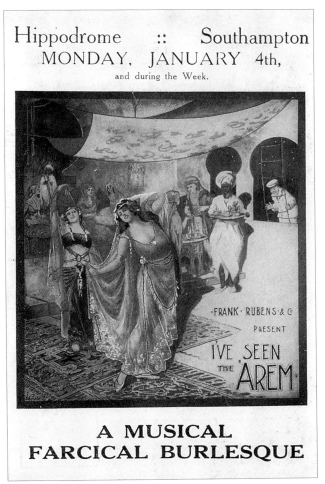

Postcard used to advertise forthcoming attractions at the Hippodrome 1910. Private collection.

In October 1913, for example, the Hippodrome devoted a week of matinee showings to "Cinema College - a Post Graduate Course in Natural History" - an "edifying, instructive, interesting" collection, with a lecturer giving detailed descriptions.

Aslatt's coach factory was demolished for the building of the Grand Theatre, opened in 1898. Notice the advertisement on the left for classes at the Philharmonic Hall. S.A.S.

In July 1913 the Grand booked a week in July for newsreels in 'Kinemacolor' - "the only system of animated pictures in the actual colours of nature". There were so many that the programmes at 7.00 and 9.00 p.m. were made "quite distinct". They included "the race for the Derby showing the Suffragette Incident", the Indian Tour of Their Majesties and the Panama Canal. The novelty of colour films evidently drew the crowds, for in December the Grand screened further 'Kinemacolor' programmes for a total of twelve nights and three matinees.

"It was called the Grand Theatre, near the Civic Centre and we used to go there and when (they put on) Shakespeare plays or the opera we used to go in the gods but we called it, to look big, the chandelier stalls...but my favourite seat in the theatre was the circle, you could look down on everybody there, the theatre prices were very reasonable; we had some lovely shows, we had the ballet every year, you had Shakespeare Company every year and you had the Grand Opera, you were well catered for in Southampton in those days."
Claire Cassie

Will Murray, resident manager of the Palace Theatre. He chose to live on the roof of the theatre in the open air with only a roof above him to stop the rain. It is not known if this proved to have the health benefits he claimed. Corbishley Collection.

"We used to go to the Grand Theatre every Saturday night, we had wooden benches to sit on in the back of the stalls."
Leslie Bradfield

"When I got married my chap took me to the Grand Theatre to see "Tarzan of the Apes" when it first came to England."
Elizabeth Saunders née Abrahams

The entrance to the Grand Theatre 1905. S.A.S.

"That was my luxury, you know. Mind you what you could do with a shilling then, quite a bit, quite a bit. The Hippodrome, you could buy a 1d. bag of peanuts. You could pay 3d. to go into the gods and if you was a smoker you could have a 2d. pack of "Woodbines" and come out and have a pint of beer for 2d. or 3d. or whatever it was. You know, so I mean, a shilling, it didn't do too bad really."
O.H.A.

"My father's sister, she was an usherette at the Palace, the old Palace Theatre, we used to get complimentary tickets and we used to go there, it was marvellous..."
O.H.A.

"The Grand Theatre, we used to have sixpence up in the gods in the Grand when we were first courting, in those days all those treats were so marvellous to us."
O.H.A.

"We all went to the Palace and while we were watching the show it came over the air that the war was over and everybody clambered on the stage, linked arms and sang songs."
O.H.A.

Other venues for occasional film showings were the pavilion on the Royal Pier and the Victoria Hall in Portland Terrace, which in 1909 became the Coliseum Skating Rink.

Besides roller skating sessions, Jacob Studt offered a range of other entertainments, including "All the Fun of the Fair" and "All the World Day by Day on the Bioscope" - all for two pence admission in 1910-11. Bioscope shows had been seen there as early as 1901, when Mr. Studt's travelling show set up its equipment, powered by a steam traction engine called "General Bullar".

Combinations of use produced problems, however. In 1913 Studt's cinema licence was made conditional upon removal of side shows obstructing exit doors; non-compliance brought a notice from the Town Clerk that it might be revoked. A temporary licence was granted subject to satisfactory reports on inspection of the premises but these seem not to have been forthcoming and the licence was not renewed.

The Borough Council could decide whether or not cinemas opened on Sundays - although in any case films could not be shown before 8.00 p.m. Licences granted in 1910 permitted such Sunday opening but when they came up for renewal in February 1911 Councillors voted against it. Following representations from the licensees of the Philharmonic Hall and the Empire, the local authority reversed its position by a majority of one vote and restored Sunday evening licences.

This position was thereafter maintained, as in 1915 when the local Free Church Council organised a 4,100 signature petition against Sunday cinemas. However, Councillors still refused to allow afternoon concerts or film shows, even if arranged in aid of charity or the Mayor's wartime Distress Relief Fund.

Some religious bodies were readier than others to use films to further their purposes. One informant remembers film shows at the Salvation Army Citadel in Newtown - with the added inducement of sweets or fruit to encourage children to attend Sunday School.

Central Hall welcomes the B.B.C. Bournemouth Orchestra.

Between the wars, Methodists in particular made good use of films. Their Central Hall off St. Mary Street, which opened on 18th February 1925, acquired a reputation as a concert hall with people like Peter Dawson and other operatic singers appearing there. The building had a projection room to show films and the remains of a projector were still there a few years ago. This was a venue where a super evening's entertainment could be had for a penny. Before the film started records

DREAM PALACES

were played and one patron remembers it was always the same tunes. A marching tune would result in the kids stamping their feet in time and the hall would shake with the din. The manager in his grey suit would climb on to the stage and request silence before the films would start. He then pressed a button which rang a bell in the operator's box and to cheers the films would start. Buck Jones, Hoots Gibson and Our Gang would all be accompanied by boos and cheers. Not a super cinema but a real one penny flicks!

"When I was a boy we used to go to the Central Hall to watch cartoons. Betty Boop and Bonzo, then we had a Church service afterwards. It cost a ha'penny and one penny to go in and we never had any money so Dad used to give us a penny and we used to go round asking grown ups to change it into two half pennies and then vice-versa. They would often let us keep both, so when we had enough money we would go to the pictures. We lived in Threefield Lane, Dad was a scaler in the docks, we used to say, 'can we go to Pictures dad?' He would say: 'there's pictures on the walls', we said 'Yes, but they're not moving', 'I'll move them for you' he said!"

Wally Chalk

When Swaythling Methodist Church opened in 1934/35 it was unusual in that it had a licence to show films to its congregation. With the influence of people like J. Arthur Rank, the Methodist movement used films to put across its religious message. Films were shown on Saturday afternoon for the children and for their parents in the evening; the Sunday evening service was followed by films. Film shows during the week were on cultural and educational subjects like travelogues and nature topics. The entrance was a small charge except on Sundays when it was free. The programmes were organised by the church members and a former projectionist remembered that the shows were presented in a very professional way.

Above Bar Street in the late 1920's with advertising poster for the Palace on left. Brazier's Archive.

STANDARD
"Cowboys, Tom Mix, Rudy Valentino and no talkies"

After the Philharmonic Hall and the Empire Theatre had turned over to films, further cinemas involved conversion of existing premises, pending sites being found for new buildings.

Advertisement for the "Latest and Best" pictures at the Standard Electric Theatre, June 1910. S.A.S.

The first, "the bottom one" of two cinemas in East Street, was created by adapting the building at 79-80 East Street, previously occupied by Baker and Co., Ltd., house furnishers. It opened late in 1909, originally styled the Picture Palace, "presenting the most interesting, amusing and instructive pictures in Southampton" at continuous performances from 3.00 to 11.00 p.m. - with the invitation "come in when you like and stop as long as you like".

Initially there were only two prices, 3d. and 6d., but after a few months they became 2d., 4d. and 6d., with special matinees for children on Wednesdays and Saturdays, 1d. only. These arrangements continued after the cinema changed hands in May 1910 and was renamed the Standard Electric Theatre, soon shortened simply to the Standard.

In 1924 it was bought for £5,000 by James Parker, who had previously owned the "Palace" at Bishop's Waltham. He refurbished the Standard, putting in a balcony and new seating for 550 patrons. Silent films were accompanied by a small orchestra. Nevertheless, the Standard remained popularly known as the "bug hutch", although not within hearing of the owner!

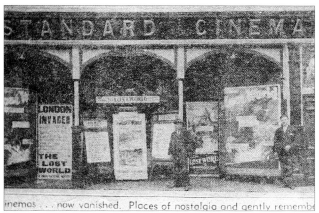

The Standard Cinema with main attraction "The Lost World" c.1925. S.A.S.

Mr. Parker's associate was a Mr. Turner who painted many signs for the forthcoming films. When *Lost World* was the main feature he painted and made up a 12ft dinosaur to put over the entrance as an advertising gimmick long before *Jurassic Park*.

The Standard closed following damage in the 1940 blitz and the building was then sold to Edwin Jones, whose own premises had been largely destroyed.

The building still stands today as a camping equipment shop and the projection box can still be seen on the roof outside, while the balcony inside is used for tent displays. The space for the projected film can be seen on the back wall by the stairs.

"Really the pictures at the bottom of East Street was only 3d. so you could go there and see the cowboys, Tom Mix, Rudy Valentino, you know, and no talkies... the lady just playing a piano and the man playing the violin... good fun... good fun... different to today."
Carlo Donnarumma

"Monday was mother's main washing day and she'd do her washing and Dad would be working in the docks. When he came home at five o'clock he'd have his tea and he used to say to mother, 'oh you go on and see your pictures', she used to follow a serial up in East Street picture house, Mondays and Thursdays, he said 'I'll clean the wash-house up for you while you're gone' and he'd meet her round the corner when she came home, she'd buy him a pint of beer."
Emily Petley, née Borrow

"We used to go to a place in East Street which was the original bug hutch, we were able to get in with jam jars, if you saved so many jam jars you could go into the cinema, you never paid any money. You'd see all the silent films …. I remember going to see Gracie Fields' first film in the town."
Edward Freestone

"When I was thirteen years old I took lessons from 'Tommy Groves'. Just before I left school my aunt spoke to Miss Elkin, who was relief pianist at the Regent and who was playing the piano at the Standard Cinema, East Street. Miss Elkin asked the proprietor, Mr. Parker, if I could be allowed to play the violin with her for the matinees, during my school holidays. I was delighted, as my ambition was to be a cinema violinist and I remember being given five shillings per week by Mr. Parker. Thinking back, the five shillings was well earned as the noisy little urchins, who came to the matinees, used to hurl monkey nut shells, orange peel and various other things over the curtain where we were playing and, sometimes, a grubby hand would try to grab my bow as it appeared over the top of the curtain, but anyway I was pleased to play in the cinema."
Eddie Dawe

"..used to go to the old Standard at the bottom of East Street, always remember, it was my first suit, and mother gave me father's watch, I've still got it to this day, one of these huge silver pocket watches with a thick silver chain, silver compass and a silver match box, you'd have the watch in your pocket and down it dangled. We were sitting in the Standard with cobwebs everywhere and there was all these tough looking hombres all around me, I was with other fellers, I suppose I was in my early teens then, and I was clutching this watch, all the way through, in fear and trepidation … as far as I can remember, it was typical, I know they called all small cinemas, and old buildings bug hutches, and it was a typical one, but we used to go there a lot and as I say cobwebs everywhere."
John Fanstone

PICTURE PALACE
"A penny each to go to the pictures"

An advertisement from May 1911 in "What's On" announces the opening of the New Southampton Picture Palace.

The cinema at the top of East Street - always advertised as being "a few doors from the High Street" - was opened on 8th May 1911 by the Southampton Picture Palace Company, which had acquired and converted a former Baptist Chapel at 113A East Street. The exterior was altered with a fancy gabled front and name board above a central pay box.

Early advertisements proclaimed "no expense has been spared to make this the most comfortable and up-to-date Theatre in the County. Tip-up upholstered seats are provided throughout and the latest ventilating, heating and sanitary appliances are installed". Continuous programmes of "the most interesting and amusing pictures obtainable" ran from 2.00 to 10.30 p.m. daily except Sundays. The 645 seats were priced 3d. and 6d. and "dainty teas were provided free of charge to all patrons occupying 6d seats at afternoon matinee".

The report of the Council's building inspector who visited both East Street cinemas around 8.00 p.m. on a Saturday in September 1911 gave a vivid account of how well they were then patronised - standing room only and excessive overcrowding of the gangways at the rear and sides of the seats. The operators were warned that their licences might be put in jeopardy, whereupon the owners of the Picture Palace undertook to allow no standing in future. For reasons of safety, the Council banned any standing in side gangways and limited it at the rear of the seats.

Mrs. Elsie King, joined the staff as a pianist in 1915 straight from school and met her future husband who was a projectionist, there. The doorman was a Mr. Harry King who looked after the black and white dog which was the cinema's "rat catcher".

The proprietor of the Picture Palace in the 1920's was Arthur Cornish-Trestrail, who afterwards ran the Wheatsheaf, Bassett, Sussex and Cowherds hotels. He raised the top price to a shilling but

Cinema staff outside the Picture Palace c.1912. S.A.S.

A more sophisticated staff group at the Picture Palace, shown on a card which the Manager, A.G. Cornish-Trestrail, sent to his regular patrons at Christmas 1921, with a complimentary ticket. Private collection.

evidently the Picture Palace found it hard to compete with higher class cinemas in the High Street and Above Bar. By 1930 it had closed. No trace of it remains, in an area that has been completely redeveloped.

"Saturday when we'd done our chores, we was given a penny each and with that penny we used to go to the pictures. The Standard at the bottom of East Street, the Picture Palace at the top of East Street, the Gaiety, and the Kingsland Square Kings Theatre. They were all a penny to go in and when you went in they'd give you an orange and a bag of sweets."
Charles Grover

"... all over Southampton (we) used to go because they used to have that many cinemas there. You used to almost go to a different cinema every night because it was really cheap you know, it was only about sixpence entrance then, sixpence, (or) a shilling."
Irene Taylor, née Becheley

KINGS (Kingsland Picture Theatre)
"It was like walking into a big cavern"

This purpose built cinema was given a civic opening by the Mayor, Alderman William Bagshaw on 8th January 1914, when the programme included the film *A Daughter of the Underworld*.

The Kings in the 1930's, with the market in full swing.

In appearance, it resembled a large shed, with a mock Tudor frontage, three false gables and a small canopy running the length of the building. Metal gates protected the entrance. At first called the Kingsland Picture Palace, it was of course, "fitted up with all the latest improvements, thoroughly heated and comfortable, with tip-up seats in all parts" - 600 at 3d., 6d., and 9d. Children were admitted at half price until 5.00 p.m. and had their special Saturday morning programmes at 1d. and 2d.

As elsewhere, afternoon tea was served free to matinee audiences... at least those occupying the more expensive seats. Patrons evidently wanted full value for money, for from March 1914 the management notified them that it "would appreciate the kindness of those witnessing the

A busy scene at Kingsland Square market. The Kings is on the left.

programme through once if the visitors would vacate their seats to make room for later patrons".

This cinema had an unusual admission arrangement, whereby the cashier receiving your money pressed a lever to deliver a metal token (instead of a paper ticket) to be handed to the usherette on entry.

Leaving the Kings on Saturday evenings, many would wait around to buy bargain meat for Sunday lunch from Kingsland Market as traders reduced prices at the end of the day - to clear stocks which they could not keep over the weekend in those pre-refrigerator days.

Over the years, the Kings featured films starring all the favourites, including Mary Pickford, Charlie Chaplin and Elmo Lincoln as the first *Tarzan*. One of the lady pianists was Mrs. Partridge who played there until the coming of the talkies. She had previously played at the Empire in French Street. Besides films, various variety acts also appeared at the Kings, accompanied by a resident orchestra.

On Boxing Day 1934 there was a bad fire in the projection box when a light fused and the flex caught fire, dropping on a film that was being re-wound. The operator, Mr. Samuel Corbishley, tried to smother the film, setting his own clothes alight; he was saved by his assistant, Mr. Walters, who returned with a fire extinguisher. Mr. Corbishley, who had been at the Kings for twenty years, suffered from burns and inhaling acrid fumes; he spent many months in hospital. For his courage, the magazine *Answers* presented him with £10 from their "Everyday Heroes" fund. He later returned to the cinema and the licence was renewed to him in 1937. The building was bombed in 1940 and remained a shell for years, becoming increasingly dangerous until the site was eventually cleared in February 1955.

"I know that when you went in you paid threepence and they gave you like a toy and a bag of sweets. I used to sneak in and I used to sneak out and go and get in the queue again which a lot of us used to do... ... I always remember there it was Roy Rogers films and that kind of thing, they had this serial going and there was one called 'The Clutching Hand'. It's ridiculous now but then in those days it wasn't. This

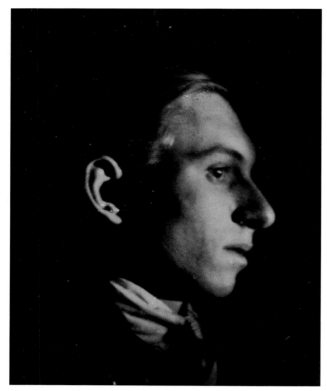
Cinema projectionist Samuel Corbishley. Corbishley Collection.

hand used to sort of come out (of) the wardrobe and get people, you know and, wow, that got me into such a state that my mother stopped me going."
Irene Taylor

"There was Kingsland Theatre Picture House where we used to go as children. Even when you grew up it was still there and that was the highlight of a Saturday afternoon as children to go there for tuppence I think it was. Father gave us a penny, mother gave us tuppence. With the threepence we'd go to the pictures and be able to buy a couple of oranges off the Kingsland Square market there...

...Gil Hulme, he used to be the dance band leader in Southampton, he ran the dances at the Royal Pier, but he was quite famous throughout the South, he was a violin player and clarinet player, but he used to accompany films at the Kings and he used to get so carried away; it was a little tiny stage, you see, with a screen but there were two pillars either side of the stage, supporting the screen, with a little sort of rostrum round the bottom of them but he used to sort of sway out over the audience and it got so hairy that they had to chain him on with a dog chain, round the back, so he wouldn't fall off!"
Sam Cooper

"It was in the afternoon. I knew a chap round in Chapel Road (who) had a greengrocery and I used to go in and sweep out and all that for him and he used to give me sixpence, and with this sixpence, sometimes we used to go... ... you saw the good films in the evening and you know they used to be 3d. and 4d. like for kids see. So I used to go to the pictures... ...and if you went to the Kings there's only two houses and if you was on the end row the screen was only about that big. You're looking up 'ere like at it. Terrible it was, till someone got up and got out. I remember there was one called 'Broken Blossoms', yeah, all the people was absolutely crying their eyes out.... 'Broken Blossoms', I'll never forget that."
Charles Grover

Reduced to a sorry state in the early 1950's, shortly before demolition. Private Collection.

"Kingsland was my main cinema, I used to go to as a kid before I left school. It was like walking into a big cavern actually, I well remember Jack the commissionaire cum general handyman cum everything, and his wife, she used to be working the ticket office and also play the piano. Where she used to go was stuck right up in the roof on a balcony and I can still see the light now and her plonking away. What we sometimes used to do - right opposite was the herbalist, Walpole, sometimes if we felt a little bit poor we used to go in there and buy some herbal mixture and smoke it in the cinema until we got caught and chucked out. A horrible stink! Old Jack used to stand in front in his uniform, they used to be protected by big iron trellis gates, Jack used to be in charge, used to have a Saturday morning rush."
Walter Olive

CARLTON
"The cosiest picture hall in Southampton"

Looking down London Road towards the town centre. c.1920. The Carlton is on the right opposite St. Paul's Church.

promotions manager for Bertram Mills Circus. His wife Violet had played piano for the silents.

"Being a silent film pianist in the old days at Southampton I can confirm that there was a cinema called the Carlton in London Road, opposite Wyntons furniture store. I played there as deputy pianist a few times in 1916, when I was sixteen years old. I was only fifteen years old when I started at Southampton Picture Palace in 1915, my first job after leaving school."

Elsie King

The Carlton, at 45 London Road, was opened on 15th January 1914 with the then sensational film *Kissing Cup*. Pictures were projected from behind the screen, for the auditorium was long and narrow, converted from shop premises previously occupied by athletic outfitters and house furnishers - flanked by butchers and grocers.

The Carlton was promoted as "the cosiest picture hall in Southampton", catering for "high class audiences", who paid 9d. or 1s. for seats in the balcony and 6d. for places in the stalls. Afternoon teas were strongly featured. Music was provided by an organist as well as "an exceedingly good lady pianist." Programmes were continuous from 2.30 to 10.45 p.m., changing twice weekly, but the Carlton made a point of not opening on Sundays. Saturday morning shows for children cost them a penny, which included a bag of sweets or an orange. For a short time in 1922 the Carlton offered live shows but it closed soon afterwards; the premises then became a car sales showroom.

The manager, Norman Young and his family lived above the cinema and when it closed he became

Front page advert for the New Carlton Picture House from "What's On in Southampton", January 1914.

IMPERIAL

Mr. Joseph D'Alesio was a shopkeeper at 11 Orchard Lane. In October 1913 the licensing authority approved his application in respect of premises at the adjoining No. 12, subject to various structural alterations being carried out. The following July a sub-committee inspected "the new picture palace in Orchard Lane", by then styled the Imperial, and confirmed the grant of a licence, still subject to certain works being satisfactorily completed.

Mr. New remembers going to the cinema on its opening day and after paying his one penny being given an ice cream cornet by Mr. D'Alesio, who was one of the Italian ice cream makers in the town. The licence stated that the building measured 18 feet by 90 feet and had iron trellis gates often associated with cinemas. It closed after a year to become a garage.

Orchard Lane, further down from where the Imperial was situated. S.A.S.

GAIETY
"A bit like a Turkish Mosque"

The Gaiety on the left in its heyday.

Of the five Southampton cinemas opened in 1914, the Gaiety was the last, not completed until several weeks after the outbreak of war with Germany. Built on the site formerly occupied by the grocers Lipton Ltd., at 169 High Street, it was designed in a distinctive semi-Moorish style, later somewhat modified.

The opening feature Loss of the Birkenhead is advertised in "What's on in Southampton", 1914.

The official opening was performed by the Sheriff of Southampton, Councillor George Etheridge, on 26th September 1914. The first programmes were exclusive showings of *Loss of the Birkenhead*, a three-part patriotic epic. October attractions included the "Great British Film Play" *Trilby*, with Sir Herbert Tree as Svengali - shown for a whole week. This was followed by *Kitchener's New Army*, "the greatest army picture ever produced".

With 800 seats priced from 3d to a shilling and Ernest Verdi as director of its full orchestra, the Gaiety was properly claimed by manager Arthur Pickup to be one of the country's best and most comfortable cinemas.

The Gaiety stayed in the same ownership from its opening in the silent film days and was later known as Southampton's first "talkie" cinema, with a showing in September 1929 of

DREAM PALACES

View of the High Street with the Gaiety up for sale in 1956. Southern Daily Echo.

Jolsons' film *The Singing Fool* for a three week season. It also showed films not booked on the major circuits and seemed to show a large number of horror films. The building was reconstructed and modernised in 1939.

Upon its demise in the 1950's the owner said "the cinema was a success in the past but owing to the cost of films and labour it could not continue as an independent house". Having survived the bombs of the war years, the Gaiety was closed on 28th April 1956; the last film was Kirk Douglas in *Detective Story*.

"Do you remember the old double seats in the Plaza, Northam? Many a nice cuddle I had there with my late dear wife. There were even more daring ones at the old Gaiety in the High Street. The back stall seats had a curtain that was a complete cover-up. One could not even see the 'movies' but those who used them were not concerned about that."
John J. Shaw

"When I became interested in music and jazz the Gaiety used to put on films the other circuits wouldn't take, lesser interest films, about jazz, music films. I've been to the Gaiety several times to see several specialist films."
Colin Brenton

"There was the Gaiety opposite East Street, that was a bit like a Turkish mosque, it had a big globe on top like a turnip with a spike on, it was a very low class place..."
Edward Simmons

PICTURE HOUSE
"Patronised by Royalty?"

Above Bar Street in the 1920's looking North. The Picture House is on the right..

The Picture House at 102 Above Bar was probably the most luxurious cinema that Southampton has had. It was situated in the main shopping area, on the site occupied today by Norwich Union House adjacent to Palmerston Park. It opened on 24th May 1920 with a programme about Ernest Shackleton's Antarctic Expedition and a Mary Pickford film. It was large by 1920's standards having 1,200 seats in the stalls (9d., 1s. and 1s. 6d.) and 400 seats in the balcony costing 2s 6d. Designed by Frank Matcham, the building was ornately decorated with pictures painted on the walls, a café and a roof tea garden giving beautiful views across the parks. The lampshades of calfskin were thought by many to be quite select. From 7.00 to 9.00 p.m. music was provided, the Director being Mr. W. G. Griggs, and a vocalist entertained. There was also a Picture House dance club offering a season ticket for 10s. 6d. and 3s. 6d. floor fee.

A cinema season ticket could be bought for £1 2s. 6d. per quarter which entitled the holder to a half crown balcony seat as often as desired. All the big silent films were shown here straight from London, including Rudolph Valentino's version of *The Four Horsemen of the Apocalypse* which climaxed with a local choral group each side of the screen singing "When I survey the Wondrous Cross". Other famous films, were D.W. Griffiths' *Orphans of the Storm* and the silent version of *Ben Hur*. A resident orchestra accompanied the films and during the afternoon a tray of tea could be brought to your seat by an attendant. When "talkies" arrived the equipment was adapted in 1929 and the first sound film, remembered by Mr. Stone, was a "shortie" of Eddy Peabody.

This popular place of entertainment continued until the blitz of November 1940 when it was bombed, the last film being *Wagons Westward*. This luxury cinema was never re-built and the site

DREAM PALACES

Usherettes, Dorothy Anne Jeffery and Ivy Severgnini in costume advertising a forthcoming film in the 1930's. Private collection.

changed in the post war rebuilding of Above Bar. The Picture House indeed catered for the local elite - but was it really entitled to advertise as "Patronised by Royalty"? If so, which member of what royal family actually attended there?

"I think the Picturehouse was generally reckoned at that time to be the top cinema in town. It had a very long foyer, you queued up outside and then you went down this long foyer and then had to queue up again, there was a queue inside almost as long as the one outside. Their big attraction was the big chandelier inside which was all lit up. It looked very posh you know...

A view of Above Bar c.1937, showing the entrances to The Picture House and Cinenews (later Classic). Private collection.

...I suppose it was about half past five, quarter to six. We went in there, bought a ticket and I sat at the back. I suppose that was 9d... and the film came on and I had been in there about half an hour... ... and on the screen they used to show the air raid warning and if you wished to leave you could do so. But no one moved ... we all sat there to enjoy the film but then the old bombs started to come down and the place started shaking and shuddering. Then the manager came on the stage and said, 'we will continue for a while but if it gets bad we will turn the lights on'. Well, they continued for a little while but it got worse and worse and you know... it was like doing a dance ... where the bombs were falling all around us I suppose. In the end a police officer came on the stage and asked us all to leave the cinema in an orderly manner, which they did do... they all got up from the front, filed their way out, and I was at the back tearing up a ticket into tiny pieces. I can still remember tearing this ticket up - I suppose I was a bit nervous. Of course they all filed out; I wasn't the last to get out. When you got outside, you never saw such a sight in your life - the whole town was on fire."
Trevor Giles

An aerial view of central Southampton. Rear of the Picture House in top right. c.1930's. Private Collection.

"And we used to go to the cinema a lot after work. It was called the Picture House ... and they had a cafe there where you had beans on toast, which seemed to be our staple diet then and cups of coffee, and we came out of the cinema - having had our beans on toast - and suddenly all hell broke loose. It sounded as though the world was coming to an end, so we staggered out on to the street. Everything was on fire and we tried to walk across the park and they had little railings of about eight inches high around the grass areas and we kept falling over these because it was the blackout and you couldn't see, except for the light of the fires. We kept falling over these on to the grass and we were in complete hysterics - laughing and crying - and not knowing if we were ever going to see our parents again. And we managed to get to the Avenue and my friend had to get to Shirley and I had to get to Bassett and I said 'goodbye' to her and she walked left to Shirley, leaving all these bombs behind and I got up to the top of the Avenue and found my father at the traffic lights, nearly demented, not knowing whether he was going to see me again."
Mary Beck

CLOCK TOWER CINEMA
"Living in another world for a few hours"

The Clock Tower Cinema was created by conversion of the building previously used by the LSWR Company - seen here on the right, opposite the Clock Tower erected in 1889 (transferred to Bitterne Park Triangle in 1934)

This was run by a father and son both named Hector Young, in a converted building at 125 Above Bar which had been the parcel office of the London and South Western Railway Company. It was a rather small cinema, providing some five hundred seats, and only operated for a few years from 1920 to 1923. Mr. Young hired out the cinema for special shows and was proud of a plastic type of seating which was easy to clean. When it closed the two projectors were sold to the Northam Picturedrome. The area has since been completely redeveloped.

"I have so many memories, very clear, though I am now in my mid-seventies, and recall the enjoyment one had in going to the 'pictures' settling in a seat with anticipation of living in another world for a few hours."
O.H.A.

"I have a distinct recollection of patronising a cinema in the early part of the century. It was situated on the corner of a cut leading to the old Grand theatre... the site was roughly an irregular triangle and the screen was at the apex end, therefore the auditorium was much wider at the rear. I know that by 1925 the site was taken over by Lloyds Bank."
A. E. Andrews. (Echo)

The building occupied by the Clock Tower Cinema was replaced by Lloyds Bank, on the corner of Civic Centre Road and Above Bar. This 1959 photograph also shows the Grand Theatre on the right. Southern Daily Echo.

EMPIRE/GAUMONT/MAYFLOWER
"The local people would get on stage and give a show"

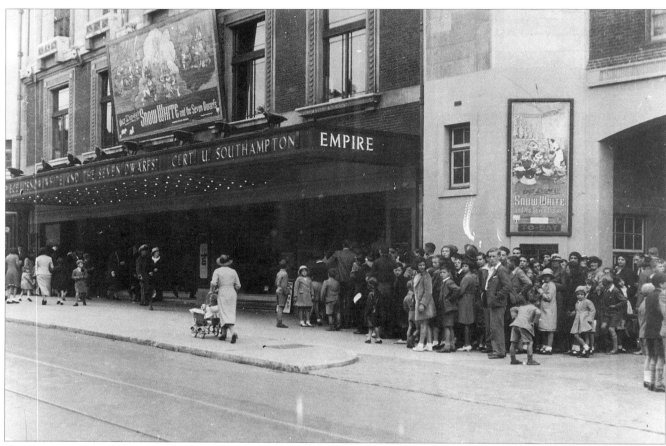

Queuing to see Snow White and the Seven Dwarfs *at the Empire, in the 1930's. Many of the grandchildren of those pictured may still be enjoying this film today. Private Collection.*

The Empire, Commercial Road, opened in December 1928 as a theatre on the Moss Empire circuit. It was one of the largest built on the South Coast with over 2,300 seats in the stalls, grand circle and upper circle. The design of the theatre was unusual in that the seating was very square to the stage, which suggests the architects had film viewers in mind. The design of the circle reinforces this as it is devoid of pillars, relying instead for support along its length by a steel girder. At the time of its construction this was the longest girder used in a theatre circle in the United Kingdom.

In 1931 it was announced that there was to be a special "talkie" season of films lasting for five weeks. These films proved so popular that they became an established feature. However, it was during the second world war that film shows really became dominant at the Empire. Before the war theatre productions usually moved from venue to venue by train. With the onset of war and the use of railways for military purposes travelling theatre productions were curtailed. Consequently Moss Empire sub-contracted their operation to General Film Distributors (forerunners of the Rank Organisation) who were showing films nationally. The Empire escaped serious damage from bombing and in the later part of the war was used as a venue for continuous film shows for troops involved in the liberation of Europe.

Eventually the theatre came under the control of the Gaumont-British film chain and the name was changed to Gaumont in January 1950. Also in 1950 big time theatre returned with performances of *Annie Get your Gun*. Throughout the 1960's and 70's the Gaumont continued to show films alongside live shows. Particularly popular were the James Bond films which played to packed houses.

Looking across Civic Centre Road to the Gaumont c.1960.

Due to falling audiences the Gaumont closed in 1986. After refurbishment it re-opened in February 1987 as the Mayflower. In 1988 it had its one and only series of films around the theme of "rock movies" such as *La Bamba*. Now established on the national circuit for large stage productions, it seems unlikely the Mayflower will be a venue for film again in the near future, having sold its projector during 1995.

"That was a 'white elephant' when they first built it. It never did as well as the others because people wouldn't go down there to Commercial Road; it was too far away from the town centre."
O.H.A.

"I decided to go to the pictures. And of course the sirens went, they got up on the stage and advised us to stay put, so we didn't have time to go outside. We could hear them ... the bombs coming down and the gas showrooms were in Commercial Road then, and I think they got hit and that was right next to the Empire. Actually they said 'would somebody like to come on the stage and entertain', and this little boy got up there with his mouth organ and I was beginning to get a little bit shaky then, because when I looked up I think the roof was on fire."
O.H.A.

"During the second world war there used to be a hole in the floor of the projection room so we could climb up instead of opening the door onto the roof and letting in the light."
Fred Smith

"If they had stopped the pictures, the local people would get on the stage themselves and give a show. I have done myself ... start singing ... anything to keep people's spirits up you see. Save them getting depressed and that often happened. We used to have some good times like that."
O.H.A.

The popular Star Wars saga continues with Return of the Jedi c.1983.

REGAL / ODEON
"Ginger the cinema cat"

Above Bar in the 1930's showing the then new Regal. Across the road is a sign advertising the Hippodrome in Ogle Road. Private collection.

The old Alexandra (ex Philharmonic Hall, dating back to 1865) was closed in 1933 and demolished, along with Scullards Hotel, to provide the site for building the new Regal in Above Bar. This was opened on 22nd June 1934 by Captain Sir Arthur H. Rostron with special guest Gracie Fields who was starring in the opening film *Love, Life and Laughter*. Huge crowds were in attendance and according to press reports at one point a mounted policeman was required to clear the street.

The super new cinema had seating for 1,700 - 2,000 in the stalls and 700 in the balcony - and included a restaurant. The Conacher organ was designed and played that first night by Reginald Foort.

The cinema was built by County Cinemas, a small circuit which also ran the Plaza at Northam. By 1937 both had been taken over by the quickly expanding Odeon chain which changed the name from Regal to Odeon in April 1945. Films changed every seven days and hold overs were very rare. In 1948, a busy year for attendances, the film *The Secret Life of Walter Mitty*, with Danny Kaye, attracted 25,000 people in one week.

In 1962 the cinema was closed for a £50,000 modernisation scheme to install new 70 mm projection equipment. The stage area was rebuilt

Sailors queue at the Regal. Private collection.

to accommodate a wide screen and accompanying speakers which produced a stereophonic effect. The interior was completely redecorated with new carpets and lighting and seats were re-arranged to give more leg room. The organ was removed piece by piece and stored in a granary on a farm near Winchester by a Mr. Tim Smith. The cinema re-opened on 7th May 1962 with a gala performance of *HMS Defiant* attended by the Mayor and guest film stars.

70mm film made it possible to produce a larger picture on the screen without loss of definition and, more important, six tracks of sound. The first was *The Robe*. followed by such favourites as *Oklahoma, Around the World in Eighty Days, Lawrence of Arabia* and *The Sound of Music*. This type of filming was very expensive and ultimately was no longer financially viable.

Royal Naval Cadets ready for inspection outside the Odeon in 1961 for opening of Sinking of the Bismarck.
Southern Daily Echo

In the 1970's audiences became smaller and the cinema closed in 1979 for a few weeks for the construction within the building of two auditoria to give patrons a choice of programme. Opened in April/May 1979, Odeon 1 provided 756 seats while Odeon 2 had seating for 576. On 9th May 1981 the restaurant closed to the disappointment of many Southampton cinema goers. This was the last restaurant run by the Rank Organisation and the loss of the tea lounge with its old style atmosphere and home cooking was the end of an era. The cinema 'treat' of Welsh rarebit, scones and jam, and knickerbocker glories gave way to another, smaller cinema, Odeon 3.

The ten most popular films at the Odeon have been:-
1. The Sound of Music - 1965
2. Oliver - 1968
3. Star Wars - 1977
4. Thoroughly Modern Millie - 1967
5. The Battle of Britain - 1969
6. Thunderball - 1965
7. Goldfinger - 1964
8. Chitty Chitty Bang Bang 1968
9. Star - 1968
10. Guns of Navarone - 1961

The management also tried other forms of entertainment with a pop show of Billy J. Kramer and the Dakotas and the Ronets in 1964 and a televised fight between Joe Bugner and Muhammad Ali in 1975. The cinema also participated in the Southampton Film Festival showing new films and including a very good Saturday morning showing of 70mm films on the big screen.

For a time rumours of the cinema facing closure circulated before the announcement came that the closing date would be 5th September 1993. Stephen Spielberg's *Jurassic Park* was the last feature.

Some of the many people who worked there were; A. E. Gilley, K. Gange, D. R. Newman-Holdsworth, G. A. Wilmot, James Tilmouth, Mrs. D. Saunders, Ms. N. Kavanagh, Mrs. Tessa Donoghe, Mabel Thompson (Mabs). One other member of the staff was "Ginger" the cinema cat, which in 1961 went missing from duty, only to reappear two weeks later. The story goes that he went to look at cinemas in Shirley and had been fed by the ladies in a chemist's shop. Hankering for the bright lights of the big city he returned to the Odeon to enjoy those Tom and Jerry cartoons and to snooze on one of the new seats.

The cinema was quickly demolished and shops were built on the site. Ironically, one of those sells videos of many of the films once shown there.

"I was an usherette at the opening of the new Regal Cinema in Southampton in 1934. I recall the visit of Gracie Fields and the crowds who came to see her perform the opening ceremony. The cinema manager

was Mr. Dunning. He had strict rules for his staff and we had to attend a daily 'inspection' to confirm that our uniforms were smart and hairstyles neat and tidy. After I had been working at the cinema for a while I asked if my sister could have a job, as an usherette. Mr. Dunning replied that he would not allow this as in his words 'relatives working together always caused trouble'. He did however, eventually relent and allowed my sister to be employed but she was to work 'upstairs' in the circle/balcony area, whilst I remained on the ground floor. I eventually became a senior usherette and on occasions relief cashier. My wage in those days was fifteen shillings per week...

...We as staff had use of the restaurant on the first floor served direct from the kitchen and our hair was styled every two weeks or so (I remember the March wave) at a hairdresser in London Road. The cinema organist I remember... seemed to play better after a 'nip of hard refreshment'."

Margery Chappell, née Chilvers

"Saturday night I hated, along the canopy, it was a very long one, they had seventy-six metal letters which picked up the light to advertise the present performance. All those letters had to be changed on a Saturday night and it was the fifth projectionists job to go down and wash all these letters in the boiler room and carry them up to the cinema, up the aisle with all the people watching the film and then I had to climb out through the restaurant window. The sheer drop, and then I had to pull all the letters out, seventy-six of them, hoping and praying that I wouldn't drop one on someone's head below because the High Street was a bit crowded in those days."

John Cooper

"Staff manager Mr. Rowe he looked after all the girls and they had a parade in the morning and they examined their hands, turned their hands over, looked at their shoes and feet, shoes and stockings...

...These ladies who go through sweeping up finding all sorts of things you wouldn't believe, they had a clearance sale, every so many months; corsets, shoes, underwear, cigarette tins, lighters, loads of umbrellas and they'd be all passed out to the staff in degrees of seniority, the best ones would have the best umbrellas .. the higher ups was the umbrellas, the other ones had the old cigarette tins...

...Somebody had been round stealing all the ladies' shoes when they took their shoes off in the cinema. They had this strange shoe fetish man who would go round picking up all the ladies shoes, and they'd be at the back in a big box all mixed up and when they came out they had to sort out all their shoes and a policeman had to be called."

Thomas Hiett

"In the very early days of the war before the blitz actually, they had, they tried out having troops in the place with a machine gun on the roof of the cinema. That only lasted for about three weeks, the troops were billeted at the back of the cinema. You know there was the old 'the show must go on' nonsense...

...When there was a good film on there were even coach trips, you know, they used to come from the country there would be trips, particularly afternoon performances, people would knock off work and their wives would be in the queue with their meals, they would eat their meals, sandwiches and flasks to go into the cinema. There were queues for the cinema, even in the blitz."

Sam Cooper

"I was eighteen and I was there with another girl, Nellie Wilcox, we used to live near each other. One week she would do chocolates and cigarettes and I would do ice cream and then vice versa and on the first Saturday night of the Blitz I didn't even know that there was an air raid on because our rooms where we used to keep the big refrigerators was right underneath the stage where the organist used to come down to get up on to the organ. And on the particular Saturday night I had done the rounds with the ice cream and I went back down round the stairs to my room and I was leaning into the 'fridge, putting the ice cream back in again, and there was an air brick above and all this dirt came in on me, I looked up and thought 'I don't know what's going on here'. I ran up round the stairs and when I went up there was pandemonium. People were crushing to get out and yet, we had had drill to tell people to go out in an orderly manner or to stay in the place. But they were going mad, treading all over each other to try and get out of the cinema you see. And we had to stay there that night and that was when they got the top half of the town."

Ada Rogers, née Gladders

Being played by its owner Tim Smith of Bursledon in 1962, the organ that once serenaded Odeon audiences. Southern Daily Echo.

"Pageboys. We stood at the door, fully uniformed, stiff shirt, collar, tie, uniform, very elaborate uniform. Tickets were paid for at the box office, then torn in half by the pageboy at the door and threaded onto a string. That was the front of house duties plus the fact you acted as a pageboy throughout the cinema for various jobs. If you had somebody else on the door then you worked in the cloakroom; you had a cloakroom attendant also delivering papers for people dining in the restaurant, numerous functions and then of course you did the labouring bit in the morning. Cleaning the ashtrays and going round and polishing the brass and windows."

Sam Cooper

"When I started there in '64 my wage was under £10, of course the value of the pound then was so much different of course. The hours, well we worked shift patterns, would be half past nine, (to) five o'clock and say from five o'clock until the close of the show, half past ten, in those days...

...The film would start, you would have adverts and trailers, an intermission of X minutes, in those days about five minutes, then you would go into your feature, your feature could be up to five, six, seven reels of possibly 20 minutes duration per reel, so of course on a six reel show you'd be doing three changeovers; at the end of the show you'd have an interval of approximately fifteen minutes as it was continuous performances. You'd go on to the next performance to repeat the previous show. You had to monitor film naturally, but that didn't mean you had to watch literally every frame projected, because that wouldn't be possible, even when you had two projectionists on duty because one would be showing one reel while one would be rewinding the previous one and lacing up the other machine...

...Yes, in those days it would have been N.A.T.K.E.Y. National Association of Theatrical, Technical, Kinematograph Employees, I think, but today the recognised union is B.E.C.T.U."

Brian Turner

FORUM/ABC
"Snogging in the back row"

The Forum under construction in 1934/35. Brazier's archive.

Exactly a year after the Regal, another super cinema, the Forum, was opened in Above Bar. It occupied the site of the old Thorner's Charity, which was demolished by the Council for the creation of Civic Centre Road to give access to the Civic Centre then being built on the West Marlands.

The ABC architect William R. Glenn designed the complex of cinema, shops and Post Office in Portland stone and multicoloured brickwork to complement the Civic Centre. In those pre-inflation days, it all cost some £45,000! The contractors, old-established local builders Brazier and Son Ltd., accomplished the main construction in only six months.

They were praised for their speed and craftsmanship by the Mayor, Councillor G. A. Waller, when he gave the Forum its civic send-off on 22nd June 1935. The opening film was *Drake over England* starring Mathison Lang and Reginald Porter Brown performed at the Compton Organ. The Forum had over 1,900 seats for which prices ranged from 6d. in the stalls to 1s. 6d. for a luxury front circle place. There were pay desks at the front of the cinema for the "dear" seats and on the Civic Centre side was one for the stalls with seating for the waiting crowds in the foyer. The cinema café offered tempting afternoon tea and snacks.

Above Bar entrance by night. 1935. Brazier's archive.

The Forum staff at the official opening in June 1935. Brazier's archive.

The stage area was 58 ft wide and 17 ft deep, with seven dressing rooms which were used when the cinema also promoted pop concerts.

During the Blitz in November 1940 the Forum was damaged when a bomb crashed through the ceiling of the auditorium, badly damaging the roof. Luckily the bomb did not explode; it was defused and by the Easter 1941 the cinema re-opened for business.

The interior of the Forum in 1935. Brazier's archive.

Braziers - who had gained a reputation as specialist cinema builders, undertaking numerous large ABC contracts - were back again in 1971 at the Above Bar cinema, which in 1959 had been renamed the ABC. Alterations and modernisation produced two separate cinemas - ABC 1 (688 seats) situated in the original circle and ABC 2 on the ground floor level with 439 seats and an adjacent lounge bar. The remainder of the stage area became a restaurant. A third screen was added in 1981 in the lounge area but did not prove very successful.

To celebrate the fiftieth birthday of the cinema a special showing of *Gone with the Wind* was arranged for invited guests. These included original staff Mrs. Betty Williams, Mrs. Jean English, Mrs. Daisy Goodall together with Jane Baxter who starred in the first film and the Brazier foreman who organised the building work.

Over half a century, the cinema screened many memorable films including first showings of *South Pacific*, *Ben Hur* and many more. Mr. Cyril Couzens was the manager here for 22 years and remembered that *Till Death us do Part* was their biggest money spinner, with *South Pacific* and *Dr. Zhivago* also very popular.

A change of ownership saw the name altered to the Cannon in November 1986. It continued until closing on 21st February 1991, consequent upon the opening of the new Cannon in Ocean Village. At present the building is being converted into a 'super pub' which amongst other attractions will have large video screens on its walls.

"There were two entrances, and two pay desks. One for the sixpennies and the front was for dearer seats. They also had that at the Atherley."
Dorothy McAllen, née Bartlett

"The Forum Cinema, that was where the organ used to come up, that was quite thrilling really when it came up all of a sudden, all lit up, all neon like he was playing from nowhere".
Pamela Humphrey, née Bowles

"(At) the Forum, they did have this little rear entrance, when I say little, it was only in relation to its front entrance, it was fully equipped, there was a cash desk there, and it was a proper entrance, well it was posher than the Roxy and anything like that, and the cheaper seats used to go in there, the sixpenny's and possibly the ninepennies at busy times, because no usherette was going to march you right down through two thousand seats from the front entrance right down to the front row. An usherette was standing inside the exit right down the front and you went in through that exit then she shone her torch on your ticket, she took you straight to the seats, her job was specifically to see to the first two or three rows and that's where I belonged. I couldn't see the beam

DREAM PALACES

The ABC seen from the Rose Garden. 1963.

from anywhere else, so I had to be down the front so that I could keep looking back from time to time."
Bert Mayell

"When we were courting, we were both very young, you could never have any privacy at home, Dad would never leave you alone, in the front room or you couldn't go anywhere really to be on your own, except the cinema. We used to love going in the back row and 'snogging' all through the film, you'd see couples all along the row doing it as well... invariably when you were asked what the film was about you didn't have a clue because you hadn't seen much of it...
Pamela Humphrey

Diary entry August 6 1950:
...Absolutely wicked weather, poured and rained all day, Sylvia and I queued for two hours to see Hotel Sahara, also Armoured Car Robbery, came home at eight, soaked, stayed up, listened to the radio and went to bed at twelve."
Pamela Humphrey

The ABC main entrance in the early 1970's. Brazier's archive.

CLASSIC
"Free milk shakes in the café"

The News Theatre under construction in 1937. Brazier's archive.

This cinema in Above Bar was originally the Cinenews, owned by Capitol and Provincial News Theatres Ltd. Their architects and the builders Brazier and Sons Ltd. were aided in the construction of the 458 seat auditorium by the slope of the land from the street to the Parks. There was a small foyer entrance at the front, leading to the auditorium which contained a small café with a pay box on the opposite side. At night the frontage was lit up by neon strip lights.

The news cinema opened by the Mayor, Alderman Harry Chick, on 12th March 1937, operated as such for little more than twelve months. It was then renamed the Classic, re-opening on 16th April 1938 when the first film was *Keep Your Seats Please*, starring George Formby. To celebrate the occasion milk shakes were free in the café!

Damaged during the Blitz, the Classic had to rely on a temporary entrance until the rebuilding of the adjacent shops several years later. As its name implied, its programmes were mainly repertory of well known films. In the 1970's a small screen built above the foyer served the little Tatler private cinema which specialised in "continental" adult films. It and the Classic closed in January 1978. Today the premises at 98 Above Bar are occupied by Burger King.

The Cinema illuminated at night. 1937. Brazier's archive.

"I went to work at the Cinenews cinema as a cashier, they showed news all day from ten in the morning until ten at night, then they changed it over to the Classic in 1938."
Dorothy McAllen

"I was in the Classic when that went... they had incendiary bombs... I was in there with my cousin. I always remember that. We came out and you used to have Burton's, the men's clothing shop on the corner and, of course, at the time when you are all running out and dog fights going on up in the sky and my cousin screaming her head off, the Burton models she thought they were bodies and there were the models laying in the park. They had been blown out. She thought they were people."
Lilian Broomfield

"The Classic was a very small cinema, and they used to have what we would call now, raunchy films, a little bit more raunchy than the normal films, but they were always about sixpence or a shilling."
Marjorie Hanley née Tucker

DREAM PALACES

After the Blitz in 1940 - the Classic suffered less damage than the Picture House.

*The staff of the Classic on closing day 14th January 1978.
Back row (left to right): Jeremy Pollard, Steve Milner (Manager), Jeffrey Pearce and Mark Coleman.
Front Row (left to right): Mrs Lil Gray, Mrs Louise Cunningham (then 74 years old and a cleaner at the cinema for 42 years), Miss Madge McGuiness, Miss Annie Pollard, Ted Austen.
Southern Daily Echo.*

NEIGHBOURHOOD CINEMAS

PICTUREDROME/QUEENS/ROXY

Northam Road c.1920, from a postcard issued by Rood Bros. The Picturedrome is on the right almost opposite St. Augustine's Church.

Built for Mr. Gough, whose family owned the nearby ice factory, this neighbourhood cinema opened in September 1914, a few weeks after the outbreak of war. Its situation, on the corner of Northam Road and Clarence Street, prompted an unsuccessful plea from St. Augustine's church against Sunday opening.

Programmes initially ran from 7.00 to 10.30 p.m., changed twice weekly and again for Sundays at 8.00 p.m. "To meet the demands of the juvenile element" there were Saturday matinees (admission one old penny). The Picturedrome contained about 500 seats, for which prices were as low as anywhere - 2d., 3d., 4d. and 6d. Audiences presumably liked what they saw. During a week in November 1914 for example, the two leading films were "a stirring dramatic Edison" *Price of the Necklace* and "the powerful thrilling drama" *The Wiles of a Siren*.

Mr. Humby was employed as chocolate seller, attendant and re-wind boy in the projection room under the operator Mr. A. Bamborough. Silent films he screened included *Curious, Broken Coin*, Elmo Lincoln in *Elmo the Mighty* and a serial *Stingaree* shown on Wednesdays.

A later owner was Captain Clements, who also owned the Regent. The Northam cinema changed its name to the Queen's Theatre in 1930, when it was bought by Mr. and Mrs. Iles for £1,200. They in turn sold it to a London company. The name was again changed, this time to the Roxy. It eventually closed in 1934 and was stripped of all its fittings to be used as a warehouse by Strides, wholesale salt merchants. The building, minus its pavement canopy, was still in use up to the 1950's, when it was demolished for re-development of the area.

"Some weeks after I left school I was in the front row at the Rialto when Mr. Hill came to me and said 'your mother wants you outside'. She had seen an advertisement for a violinist at the Picturedrome, Northam. We got on the tram to Northam and I saw Mr. Bisner, the proprietor. He arranged an audition the following day, with two other players. I got the job. My ambition was realised...

...I well remember those days. Miss 'Billie' Eadie was the pianist; she was a very nice girl of around 18. Then there was Mr. Archie Bamber, the Manager - cum - operator; his wife Dolly used to be in the ticket box. Also there was Fred Webb, he used to be the

general 'dogs body', cleaning, painting and relief operator. Very soon the talkies came and that was the end of my cinema days. My musical career later was with Gil Hulme's band."
Eddie Dawe

"Now the Roxy you could berate that as a flea-pit, bug hutch, or what, but to me that was a little treasure, it was only small, very intimate and the projectionists obviously loved their job, to me the show was as good as you'd see anywhere "
Bert Mayell

"There was also the time, when I was younger we used to go to Northam pictures, that was the old Roxy. Well you could imagine on a Saturday afternoon, it used to be tuppence in those days, a penny a picture, and we used to get a penny monster - now that was bottles, in those days, with a little marble in, glass marble, and I can remember you had to press the marble down and once you pressed the marble down by the rubber then gas would be released, you know... and when we emptied those bottles, I can still remember, running them down the aisle in Northam pictures, you know the sloping aisle like that, you'd get about three or four of them rattling down in all the picture... that was the old silent days... and right near the front. Just in front of the screen they used to have a curtain go round and an old piano there and a pianist playing which kept the music for the film, whatever it was, and I often thought to myself, thinking back, that woman playing that piano must have had an umbrella up, because all the peels used to go there and all kiddies like that, oranges and all the peel used to throw over there. How she used to play the thing I don't know. I think the lights used to go up about once every ten minutes and we'd get threatened and all thrown out if we didn't keep quiet and that was the days of old Pearl White and we used to shout out 'look who's behind you, look who's behind you', you can imagine the kids, can't you and the uproar was terrific..... when we got too bad the old manager used to put the lights up telling us all to keep quiet otherwise he'd throw the lot of us out. Well it did keep us quiet for a few minutes but it was impossible and... but those were the days, there's no doubt about it."
George Cook

"... at the Roxy on a Wednesday afternoon was a penny. One penny and if it was a love film they'd all stamp their feet. All the chaps would...' and then the man there he had a couple of sons, he'd put the light up (and) he'd come up the front and say he'd clear the place. Then all the old orange peel and apple stuff used to go over at him and there would be this chap playing the piano or girl playing the piano it was often a girl, and they used to throw it all over the top and that was the good old days!"
O.H.A.

Children of Rochester Street, Northam in 1925.

"We had Saturday morning matinees at the Roxy, tuppence - and it wasn't very good. Old Westerns - and you'd get the kids calling out 'look behind you mister'. You couldn't hear what was being said."
O.H.A.

"The dear old Roxy would do a two day programme and a separate show on Sunday, and those boys really earned their coins there, they wouldn't be getting much because they only had a two hundred, three hundred seater and I used to sit in there on a kid's matinee, two on a seat, you would have thought they'd been put in with a shoe horn, two small ones together, you know, lovely, it really was very very nice."
Bert Mayell

"Matinees, you had the children's matinees, used to walk from Bitterne down to Northam to one of the cinemas there, it was probably the Roxy, I think, and I always remember that; it was a pretty tough area in those days and we used to sit in a group from Bitterne, and I remember they used to put a number up on the screen, lucky number, if you had a ticket as you went in, you had a prize, and I won it one week and it was a rabbit, and I clutched this rabbit and I think we ran from Northam to Bitterne with several Northam yobs trying to catch us..."
John Fanstone

PLAZA
"The illuminated Compton Organ"

The Plaza, October 1932.

The Plaza on Northam Road, was one of the finest of the many super-cinemas built in the 1930's. Large amounts of money were spent on its fixtures and fittings and the luxurious image was heightened by a facade of white stone illuminated at night by three colour floodlights. It also had the added attraction of a car park, rare for cinemas of that era.

It was opened on 11th October 1932 by the Mayor, Fred Woolley, for the owner Mr. J. G. Sprinkernell. Its opening film *Looking on the Bright Side* starred Gracie Fields.

The entrance hall was large and lofty, decorative and well lit, leading to two broad staircases to the stalls and balcony, where hundreds of patrons could wait to enter the cinema. The seating was very comfortable, with good views of the screen from anywhere in the building. The back row double seats will be remembered by many people who did their courting at that time. Everything from the ticket machine to the heating and ventilation was operated by electricity. There was also an illuminated Compton organ (one of the world's first) played by Leslie James and later by Leslie Holman as resident organist.

The Foyer of the Plaza, 1932.

The Interior of the Plaza.

This 2,100 seat cinema - a credit to its architect Robert Cromie - was controlled in 1934 by County Cinemas Limited who also built the Regal but was absorbed into the Odeon chain in 1937.

The children's Saturday morning club was called the "Mickey Mouse" club and children were often entertained by Ken Batten, the Chief Projectionist, who played the organ for them, in addition to screening the serial, cartoon and main feature.

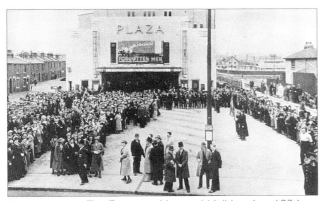
Queuing to see The Forgotten Men and Helldorado c.1934.

The Plaza started as a first-run cinema but soon changed to a split week of three days, three days and different films on Sundays. The proscenium width of 30 feet was a great advantage when the cinema was adapted for Cinemascope, many thinking this was the best installation in town.

With the decline of cinema-going the Plaza closed on Saturday 30th November 1957 but the building was not demolished. Its interior was gutted and into the empty shell were built two studios, dressing rooms and offices for Southern Television, which went on air 30th August 1958.

By coincidence Gracie Fields starred in the first show for television as she had in the opening film of 1932. Later, when new studios were built, the building was demolished and an office block built on the site.

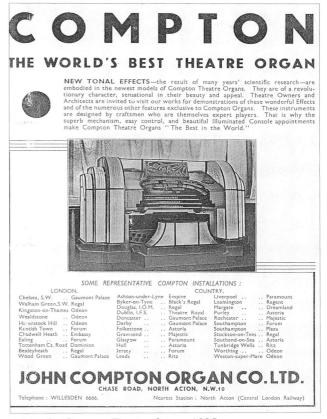
Advert for Compton Theatre Organ, 1935.

"Then they built the Plaza. At the Broadway, we had seven days a week, never a day off and it was rumoured around that there was a day off, we had ten shillings a week and the Plaza was paying a pound, so naturally we queued up, most of the cinema usherettes were queuing up, I got the cashier's job there and stayed there until I was married in 1935...

...I was working during the opening in 1932. I shall never forget that because being a cashier it was all free seats or guests so there was nothing for me to do that evening so they put me in the cloakroom and I was there 'till about two in the morning...

...When I worked at the Plaza, we had to go on parade before we went on duty, looked up and down make sure our seams were straight..."
Dorothy McAllen

"I remember going to the Plaza, they had a juggler and an organ; the organ used to come up out of the floor...

...There was double seats in the back of the Plaza... ninepence, one and thruppence and one and six for the back seats, something like that, they were very popular was the double seats."
Thomas Hiett

Plaza Doormen in the 1930's.

"I know I started off there in '44, as a re-wind boy, which was the lowest of the low; you re-wound the films when they came off and put them back in the containers and they'd be ready for the next showing. Laced up the machines as they called it, put the films in the top spool box and down through the sprockets and ran it down far enough so that when the chap started it up on the machine ... but that was the re-wind job anyway, so you sort of progressed then to third operator. I had no training in this job; you know you were expected to do all sorts of things...

...We used to share the news reels as most of them shared a newsreel with their sister cinema, I think the Forum and the Broadway, so the Paramount news from the Plaza was shared with the Odeon in the High Street, when the news had finished, it was reeled off and put into a big box about eighteen inches square, a metal box, a proper built container, fireproof, hopefully, and I'd just go across the road with it, wait across by the cottages at the other side of the road for the bus going into Southampton, get off the bus at the corner of Pound Tree Road, usually hop off the bus there before it went on down Pound Tree Road, and then take it off up into the projection room, wait until they'd spooled it off and showed it and then bring it back to the Plaza, on the bus...

... opposite the cinema there is a row of terraced cottages, where the midwife, Nurse Buckett used to live, and frequently during a film, when she was wanted for a delivery, we had to put a slide up on the screen and ask her to report to the pay desk...

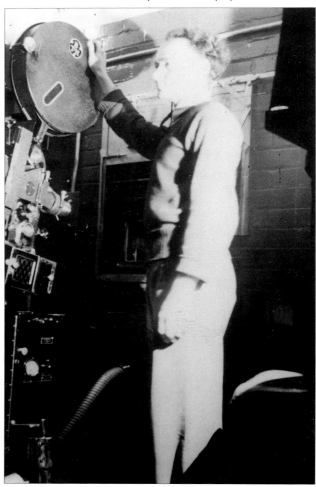
Thomas Wheeler, Projectionist at the Plaza. c.1940. Private Collection.

"At the Plaza, we would often have a practice run with new films, as the Chief was a perfectionist and he would not tolerate any sort of technicality during the actual show. Everything was done to run smooth as it should from opening and closing two massive sets of curtains. The correct fading for screen lighting and of course sound level, which he would set according to the audience capacity and correct lighting from the projectors to the screen. The correct use of the spotlight for the ice cream girl and the organist and not forgetting the air conditioning in the auditorium. I was trying to remember if it was Ken Batten that I worked under, but cannot confirm this, it's a long time ago, but we had a staff of five projectionists in those days, including Curly, we all worked as a team and enjoyed it. However, I can assure you no one touched the projectors until the Chief knew you were ready so he was very cautious with the apprentices and rightly so, when you consider the equipment involved, just like Rolls-Royce where if you do not appreciate and respect what you are working with then you are not the person to be around such equipment."
Thomas Wheeler

Plaza staff including (back row from right to left): Len, Bill Cooper, Colin Brenton (all projection room staff) c.1944. Private Collection.

"...I mean the conditions, I don't know what they're like in the cinema now, but they really weren't very good, but having said that they were happy days, you know, I mean I never forget the days in the cinema they were really good, but the wages just weren't very good, I mean, then I didn't bother about my wages, it probably wasn't any more than five or six pounds a week, something like that, we're talking about '44, my father was earning a lot more money than that then, he was doing wartime work in the docks as a shipwright you know...

...The Plaza was in quite a rough area and there were problems, the early forms of vandalism, I mean the toilets used to get ripped up at the Plaza and that's going back to the forties, early fifties and the exit doors were frequently prised open and crowds would come charging in; the police really didn't want to know about it, they used to say well, you know, get them in the exit and do them over and get rid of them, and that was it, and that's what we used to do most of the time, but there were problems there...

...Just one other amusing incident I can just recall from the days when I worked at the Plaza. The staff room then was above a railway siding where they used to park up the trucks loaded with peanuts that were bound for the margarine factory which was just across the other side of Northam Road and on one occasion I can remember lowering a bucket down from the staff room to these trucks that were just underneath and somebody got out and you just had to lift the tarpaulin up slightly and you could just load the bucket up with peanuts and pull it up to the top; didn't happen very often, you had to watch there was nobody about but it was very convenient because it was just immediately below the staff room window, that's the thing I can remember doing a couple of times, very nice peanuts."

Colin Brenton

SCALA/LYRIC
"Frankenstein, Dracula and the Mummy!"

The Scala/Lyric (1914 - 40) at St. Denys near Cobden Bridge.

The building is commodious and comfortable, an uninterrupted view of the screen being obtainable from all parts, while tip-up seats are provided throughout. An adaptation of Thomas Hardy's novel Tess of the D'Urbervilles, with its absorbing interest and variety of incident, proved much to the liking of the large number of picture-goers who visited the Scala upon the opening day." Thus the Southampton Times enthused about the opening on 6th April 1914 of "the new picture palace which Bitterne Park and St. Denys can now boast as having for their own." The purpose built Scala in St. Denys Road, near Cobden Bridge had a glass awning to shelter patrons waiting to see its "long and varied programmes" screened twice nightly (6.30 to 10.30 p.m.) and also on Saturday afternoons and Sunday evenings. There were 550 seats at 2d., 4d., and 6d.

The name was changed to the Lyric in 1926, when a new manager improved amenities by reducing the seating to 410; prices then ranged from 5d. to 1s., but later became "all seats 6d" (2½p) in the 1930's. The Lyric continued showing films until wartime conditions brought about its closure in 1940. The building was afterwards used as a warehouse for a pharmacy business, later Guttering Services and Sovereign Bathroom Centre.

"The Lyric was a little, tiny, bug hutch, not a circuit cinema, just a little, tiny, private cinema I should imagine, but it used to be well patronised... it was a cheap evening, it was about thruppence or sixpence, no balcony, double seats up the sides for courting couples."
Eric Martin

"I think I must have been about twelve when I went to the Lyric, round about the early 30's, all silent films, they used to have a pianist. We used to go down Lances Hill, across the step stile and up Monks Path to the top end of Midanbury Lane and Cobden Avenue and then across the Bridge into the cinema. The Manager was a disciplinarian, he used to carry a long ruler or a baton and go up and down the aisle and try and keep the children in order."
Bill Hulbert

"I used to go to the Lyric too, at St. Denys, I used to go there on my own quite a lot or with other lads, that was our way of life in those days, used to go to them all, Palladium, Broadway. Didn't often go to the big ones I remember, don't know why; funny that, thinking back, we used to go to them occasionally, but I suppose we kept that in reserve for when we went with our families."
John Fanstone

"Oh it was a very, very small place, (we) used to call it the flea pit or the bug hutch I know that wasn't the original one, the flea pit was the one in East Street, which I don't remember really, but the Lyric was small. It had on the roof, which I could see from my bedroom window in Castle Road, 'all one price, 6d.', in great big block letters on the roof. The sort of films they used to show there were a lot of the H category films, you know, the Frankenstein, Dracula films, came into the category, the Mummy, that sort of thing."
Colin Brenton

PALLADIUM
"Flicker-free projection"

Wounded soldiers and Belgian refugees attending a show at the Palladium during World War 1. Private Collection.

On the 3rd May 1958 the Palladium closed its doors after 45 years of serving the public through many changes in forms of cinema entertainment.

For its civic opening on 17th February 1913, the Mayor, Mr. Henry Bowyer, was supported by a bevy of Council and other VIP's. The Palladium was then described as "the prettiest picture palace south of London". Its walls were decorated in Wedgwood style, matching the blue plush seats - 150 in the balcony, 500 stalls. With balcony seats costing 1s. (bookable in advance for 3d., extra) the Palladium aimed at "select" audiences - to whom it offered "flicker-free" projection, "perfect ventilation" by three electric fans, with the safety factor of "ample exits" to allow the whole cinema to be safely emptied in under two minutes.

Its showing of *Antony and Cleopatra* for a whole week in January 1914 - advertised as "The Most Gorgeous Creation in the World of Cinematography; cost of production alone £40,000" - exemplified its "high standards and distinct educational values".

The Palladium in the 1950's. Private Collection.

It was a popular cinema handily sited opposite the tram depot - and is remembered by many for its glass canopy which covered all the pavement for the length of the cinema and the sweet shops. The word "cosy" was often used to describe the interior. During its opening year the cinema tried a sound system using a record intended to synchronise with the film but this was unreliable and soon discontinued. Like the Atherley, the Palladium entertained French and Belgians during World War I and also put on shows.

At the time it closed it was managed by Mr. B. L. Mayer, who also ran the Savoy at Swaythling; the patrons were invited to go there instead. The film *Murder at St. Trinian's* was the last to be shown in 1958. The building was subsequently altered to become a supermarket. The frontage was completely changed and today gives no indication that it was one of our earliest cinemas.

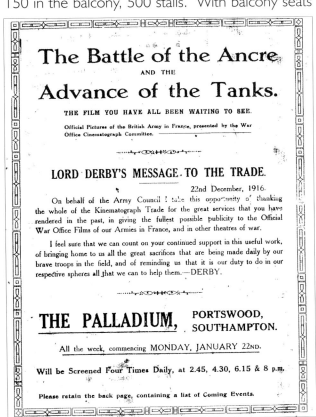

Advertising for newsreels in 1917. Private Collection.

DREAM PALACES

The Palladium in 1958 when the main feature was A Tale of Two Cities - "a modest but still costly remake" starring Dirk Bogarde. Southern Daily Echo.

"When the Palladium Cinema was built in 1913 a sweet shop was opened on the same premises. It was originally called 'The Mikado' and the woman who ran it always dressed up in Geisha costume, wig and all. It later changed hands and became the 'Chocolate Box'."
O.H.A.

"We went to a film at the Palladium in Portswood, my mother and sister went first and they came home absolutely full up, they'd seen my brother on film in France (First World War) with his two horses, he was laughing all over his face and they said 'cor, that's our Bert', they couldn't get over it and we all had to go one after another to see our Bert on the film, because I mean films were just in their making then, they weren't very popular, I mean to go and see your brother on the films was absolutely marvellous...

... I went to the Palladium when it first opened. I was about ten then (1913) it was one penny on Saturday morning. I went to one down town, me and my sister went to town to fetch a joint, father used to get the meat down town and we used to go and fetch it and we thought we would go into the pictures. We were all the afternoon trying to find our way in. We went in, we went up and we went round and they were coming out by the time we found where we had to go in, we'd spent our pennies and we had to walk all the way home then. Father used to give us a penny to come home by tram and we used to spend our pennies and walk home and we hadn't seen the film we went to see."
Joyce Hare

"The fact that we lived at Bassett, Swaythling, the Palladium was the favourite one, it was sixpence or a shilling in the downstairs and my husband's mother and father used to go there Tuesday and Thursdays and down the front on the left hand side the last row of the shillings. They were so well known in there they

48

eventually had their names put on the seats, Sara and Jim. When they pulled the Palladium down we tried to get the seats, but they were gone."
Marjorie Hanley

"I saw the manager Mr. Mayer in the Palladium and we went through the usual proceedings and what the job was, ... the operating box was downstairs it wasn't upstairs in the Palladium. It was all dark and there was a lot of noise, a lot of sound from the speakers in the operating box and the machine was rattling away, and just as I went in the door the change over was going on, there was lots of bustling because one machine was just finishing and the other one was just starting; they were 70mm reels. You trained under the supervision of the other projectionist, you were not allowed, in those days, on the machines until you'd really been in the operating box for at least six months. Apart from cleaning it you weren't allowed to touch it. The projectionists above, two of them got called up, so actually I was only a rewind boy for nine months... mind you I must have taken an interest in the job because they said I was competent enough to take over the running of the machine so that was luck really, so I stepped up to a third projectionist first of all and then a second. I was fifteen and in charge of all of the equipment like and the cinema job, I dunno, it used to get to you to show films, up there, entertaining people like. When you had a day off you would go to the cinema, to other cinemas, because the Palladium and Savoy were sort of second rate cinemas. They didn't get the big musicals like the Odeon or ABC. Mr. Mayer was the Manager at the Palladium, a nice old chap, lived round in Grosvenor Road. He was an old cinema projectionist himself from the silent days. I think the Mayers used to be circus people."
Eric Martin

"When I was about sixteen, I had my first kiss in the cinema, can't even remember the film, we were in the back row and the arm came round the back, and I didn't know quite what to expect, I think there must have been a lull in the film and I can remember him pulling my face round with his hand and this big smacker, nowhere near the smackers of these days oh, it was wonderful, absolutely wonderful, courting was a lot different in those days, I'd known him since I was ten."
Marjorie Hanley

BROADWAY
"They were stars then"

Broadway c.1962. The main feature was Tamahine starring Nancy Kwan as the "glamorous Polynesian cousin of a boys' school headmaster". Southern Daily Echo.

This cinema's design suggests a castle and today it still catches the eye, contrasting with the other buildings in Portswood Road shopping centre.

This was Mr. W. D. Buck's second cinema (see Atherley) but it passed into ABC control in 1936. The 1,546 seat cinema was built by contractors Wilson Lovatt and Sons on a site that sloped quite steeply from the road, which helped in constructing the auditorium. The stalls sloped from a relatively high stage to a rake of stadium-type seats with a balcony above and four boxes at the back. The decor had suggestions of King Arthur and Camelot with wood panelling and plasterwork painted to resemble squared stonework. On each side wall there was a painting of a knight riding a horse carrying a lady, towards a Disney-like castle.

The first manager was Mr. Ronald Buck who on the opening night of 6th June 1930 welcomed the guests including the Mayor, Mr. Hector Young, to see *Rookery Nook* starring Ralph Lynn and Tom Walls.

There was a small restaurant for snacks and a local dance band led by Brian Gorman played on Sunday evenings. On the walls outside the cinema, where the audience queued, you can still see names scratched in the brickwork.

The Broadway survived the War undamaged and was well known for showing the magnificent MGM musicals. However, the slump in cinema-going in the early 1960's led to its closing on 26th October 1963. It then reopened as the Broadway Bingo Club. Apart from the floors being levelled, few alterations were made and today the building still looks very much like a cinema.

"I don't remember going to the cinema, to the Broadway, with my mother; it was always my father. We used to call in (at) a little sweetshop along Portswood and used to buy this bar of plain York chocolate or some particular sweets... ...then from there we took a few steps along to the Broadway and there were times there, I saw the 'Elephant Boy' there, and I don't know what it's like in the Broadway now but along the side then they had sort of murals either side and I often remember these animals that were on there, thinking you know, were they real? I was only about seven or eight then. That's my earliest recollection of the Broadway, the Broadway was the first cinema that I went to."
Colin Brenton

"When the Broadway was built, we used to go quite a bit, it was a huge great big place .... well, we thought it was ... and you went down towards St. Denys and there was another little cinema on the left and I think it was called the Savoy, and they had double seats in the back row, that was another favourite."
Marjorie Hanley

"They were stars then, they weren't like they are now, they were film stars, you didn't know all the sleaze about their lives. Where you can read everything now, to us they were idols of the screen and you loved them and looked up to them, it's really surprised us that all these years we never knew that big tough guys (often) were gay...

...We would go about three times a week; where Southampton was devastated after the war, there was virtually nothing to do... the cinema was somewhere you could go with your boyfriend and have a snog... you were warm as well..."
Pamela Humphrey

PLAZA HALL, PORTSWOOD ROAD

Was this a cinema? Several people claim to have seen films here. It was built in 1929 by Mr. Ernest Whyte and his brother, a bassist and violinist who were involved with the entertainment business. It was certainly a dance hall, where a group called the Melody Five played in 1930 - 1936, and was called the Plaza Ballroom in the 1940's. Mr. Fryer remembers seeing *Dick Turpin's Ride to York* there with the sound of the steam trains rumbling by the back of the building.

While films were evidently shown at this hall, the occasions were probable few - and "private", since there is no record of the premises being licensed for cinema use.

In the 1950's it was used by Oddie Fasteners as a warehouse and later changed hands, to become the first B and Q, DIY store in the country. There was no sign of a projection box, although there was a balcony. All was destroyed in a fire in the early 1990's.

SAVOY
"I suppose you called it courting"

The Savoy Cinema, Swaythling. Southern Daily Echo.

The last of Southampton's newly built pre-war cinemas was the Savoy, in High Road, Swaythling. It was officially opened by the Deputy Mayor, Councillor G. E. H. Prince, on 10th November 1938, when the first film shown there was *Jezebel*, starring Bette Davis and George Brent.

The Savoy, designed by H. Colin Farmer and built by A. G. Saunders Ltd. for Louis Zeid, had a main structure of brick and a cream tiled front with a feature made of the projection box. A small foyer led to the auditorium and a balcony which gently vibrated when a heavy train thundered along the nearby line.

The Savoy originally had 1,505 seats, later reduced to 1,032. These became increasingly difficult to fill and the last showing of *Bridge on the River Kwai* on 28th March 1959 was followed by closure and demolition. It was proposed to build a block of flats to be called Savoy Mansions but these never materialised and a garage took over the site.

"We used to go round in a crowd, to the cinema, girls never paid, the boys always paid for them and we, I suppose you called it courting, we were about sixteen or seventeen."
Marjorie Hanley

SHIRLEY ELECTRIC
"Jessie Balderson the Musical Director"

An advertisement from "What's On" on the opening of the Shirley Electric Theatre. 1910.

The Foresters' Hall in Park Street was taken for the 1908-9 winter season by the Picture and Variety Company but details of its programmes or any other earlier film showings in Shirley are elusive. The first regular cinema on the west side of Southampton was the Shirley Electric Theatre, which opened on Boxing Day 1910.

"This newly equipped and comfortably furnished picture theatre" was housed in a corrugated iron building erected in Shirley Road between Shirley Avenue and Howards Grove. It was styled the Electric from the outset, although early licences were issued in the name of the Picturedrome, to Jury's Imperial Pictures Ltd, They alliteratively advertised "Jury's Joyful and Judicious Pictures Perfectly Presented" - accompanied by "Jury's Bijou Orchestra".

The seating was for 800 but one patron recalled that there were a lot of forms and one push could topple the rest with them all ending up on the floor. The prices in the evening were 2d., for front seats, 6d., in the middle and 9d., for back seats and balcony. For 2d. and 1d. you entered the cinema from the Howard Grove entrance. Children were not allowed in on an evening (6.30 to 10.00 p.m.) unless accompanied by an adult.

Classics like *Hiawatha, East Lynne, Uncle Tom's Cabin* and *Quo Vadis* were popular. They were accompanied by the theatre orchestra under the direction of Jessie Balderson.

The first big serial was *The Million Dollar Mystery*, this ran for 20 weeks and its star Richard Harris came from America and appeared on the stage in his cowboy outfit, riding a horse. Other serials included the *Master Key, The Broken Key* and *Son of Tarzan*.

During World War One the Electric was taken over by Mr. A. Gough. The Armistice was celebrated with a dinner for the staff. Their jobs

Jessie Balderson. Musical Director at the Electric. Private Collection.

ended in 1922 when the Electric closed down. The building was used as a second hand furniture store before being demolished to make way for the present Gordon Buildings.

"The Shirley Electric, belonging to the Jury's group, was known to we kids variously as 'Jury's', ' The 'Bug Hutch', 'The Tin House' but never as 'The Glory'. It was a corrugated iron building. The Atherley was built in 1912 and was rather a better class palace but we youngsters used to like Jury's better because the films had more rough stuff in them, and the Atherley had more love yarns."
W. A. Hawkesworth. (Echo)

"How well I remember those days, especially so for me as my Aunt Jessie Balderson was the Musical Director at the Shirley Electric cinema during part of the first World War and, I think, up until about 1920. At this time my Mother and my aunt shared a house in Shirley and I was fascinated when my Aunt used to play the piano. She was a very gifted musician".
Eddie Dawe

Shirley High Street, Electric on the right. Private Collection.

Shirley High Street, Electric on the left.

THE ATHERLEY
"The best tuppence worth in the world"

Interior of the Atherley 1912.

Until 1912 all the films seen in Southampton were screened in converted buildings which had previously served various other uses. It was easier to find sites for new buildings in the suburbs rather than the town centre; hence Southampton's first purpose-built cinema was the Atherley at Shirley - given the name of the distinguished local landowners whose estate was then being built over.

The Atherley Cinema Theatre, as it was first called, resulted from the enterprise of a local builder William Dalton Buck (1878-1966), who became interested in cinemas and decided to invest in building one himself. He made a good job of it!

Opened on 14th September 1912, with the films *Their Golden Anniversary* and *The Fatal Mirror,* the Atherley initially contained 650 seats, priced at 3d., and 6d., in the stalls and 9d., in the balcony; also 2d., 3d., and 4d., for the Saturday morning children's show.

During the 1914-18 War, Mr. Buck used to entertain Belgian and other Allied convalescent soldiers from the Red Cross Hospitals in Regents Park to afternoon shows at his cinema, collecting and returning them in his car.

His cinema venture proved gratifyingly successful and he later went on to engage in a second, opening the Broadway at Portswood in 1930. Mr. Buck also gave his time to serve as a borough councillor for Shirley from 1921 and was Mayor in 1933-34.

The success of the Atherley led him to enlarge it in 1919 by adding a new wing. The sight lines for the audience were altered and the main hall was lengthened for the new screen position, as can still be seen today by the different coloured bricks on the side wall in Malmesbury Road. The capacity was increased to over 1,000 seats. Many of the great films of the silent era were premiered here and Mr. Buck, when celebrating his Diamond Wedding in 1961 said, "Charlie Chaplin made the Atherley for me. They used to flock to see him."

A major event at the Atherley on 15th July 1929

The Atherley in 1961. The main feature is the Cinemascope film The Young Ones, starring Cliff Richard.

Jack Dalton Buck, aged 21 years in 1930. He was Manager of the Atherley which his father William had built.
Private Collection

was the first showing of a full length talking and singing film called *Lucky Boy*. The film starred George Jessel who had turned down the role in the *Jazz Singer* eventually played by Al Jolson. The new sound system was a great success and crowds flocked to experience the new phenomenon.

In the 1950's the Atherley became the first in Southampton to embrace the new developments of Cinemascope and stereophonic sound, with a showing in February 1955 of *The Robe*. The cinema stage was altered to allow three speakers behind a 38ft. wide screen, with 24 other speakers mounted around the hall. The seating was altered and 100 seats lost to give better viewing for this new wide screen. Indian, Chinese and Greek films were shown here, as were specialist seasons on opera and ballet. The Atherley also provided a home for the Southampton Film Society. Films were shown for the last time on Saturday 15th November 1975, after which the building became a venue for Bingo. At one stage it was planned to

retain a small 150 seater cinema in the circle but unfortunately this did not happen. The balcony area was converted to offices with a separate entrance and the interior was decorated for use as a bingo hall. The canopy which used to shelter the waiting cinema-goers was removed and a smaller decorative one replaced it. Externally, the building still looks like a silent picture house.

"I was born in Shirley Road (in) 1909. My father started to build the Atherley cinema in 1911 when I was about two, two and a half. I used to push this little wheelbarrow my father bought me, used to put a few bricks in it and then be left to take them out, go up ladders and he had a black retriever dog that used to follow me up the ladder, I can remember all this very well. Dad was apprenticed at Braziers, the builders and his father also was apprenticed at Braziers; he was quite a good builder, build quite a few houses, then decided to build a cinema himself... ...he saw a small cinema show in East Street, and he thought 'I'll build a proper cinema' so his was a

cinema built for films, he was a very far-seeing man. My mother was a pianist so when Dad started the cinema she used to work out the scores with Charlie Poland, first violinist, and then there was an organist Mr. Payne and a double bass. At fifteen I was allowed to do the effects which were quite funny in those days, rolling peas in brass drums for rain, cymbals for lightning, blank cartridges for Tom Mix cowboys, it was quite amusing, the crowd used to love it. My sister was in charge of the usherettes, we used to have about ten, whereas you go down the big one at Ocean Village and you walk in there on your own in the dark! We used to have about ten girls and my sister used to be manageress and she also ran the sweets, chocolate and ice cream. We used to have queues all round the cinema down to past our house which was at the back of the cinema and we'd open up about quarter to six, we'd have a matinee on Wednesday afternoons and a children's matinee on Saturday afternoons which we used to charge tuppence for... a straight figure, not fourpence or anything like that, tuppence and it's amazing, when I went to Lloyds bank, well a year or two back, Mr. Philips was there, the manager and he said to me are you the Jack Buck who used to take tuppence off me when I was a (kid). He still never gave me a bigger overdraft! I always wore evening dress... and I talked to people when they came in and went out. I remember one woman, we used to put on two films and a news, sometimes a cartoon, I remember one woman coming in and saying 'Mr. Buck, no Mickey Mouse this week?' as she paid her shilling. Two films, a cartoon and a news. Later on I took on Brian Gorman and his band and he had a very good crooner called Bert Sewell who went to croon for Ambrose afterwards and the crowd loved that. What the crowd did laugh at was when the films used to break down; when talkies first started we used to be given a disk, like ordinary records and you started the film the same time as the disk. Slight little hiccough, they were talking in front of us or all behind and of course this was great fun for the audience, they loved it, they clapped and cheered! They were quite upset it you kept it going well!"
Jack Buck

"Oh hilarious wonderful, It was great, the best tuppence worth in the world, you could wander out, go to a cinema your mum gave you tuppence and you went in and there was no fear of being molested or mugged except probably the kid in the seat behind he'd stick glue in your hair or something like that! Those posh kids that could afford ice cream would be up in the balcony in the thruppenies. and melt their ice creams and pour it on the radiators and pour it on us paupers down in the stalls during the interval Generally speaking there was all the cheering and there were the inevitable serials, everyone went to the serials, Flash Gordon and Tailspin Tommy, you get a sort of ten minute episode and the guys going to be thrown over the cliff; you go along and you think how the hell's he going to get out of that and then next week go along and he wasn't thrown over the cliff, he'd got up and the other guy behind him had missed. Great. We went along in great groups."
Sam Cooper

"My grandfather, my mother's father, he was a Chief Engineer torpedoed three times in the first World War, but he couldn't swim! They didn't have pensions in those days so my father gave him a job when he retired, screwing up the seats, keeping them all tight at the Atherley cinema and it was quite funny, there were two seats in the middle of the sixpennies, right in the middle, on their own with nobody in front of you. People used to queue up for those two seats, get there at half past five and wait for an hour for you to

Converted for Bingo but still retaining its original doors in the 1980's. Private Collection.

open, they'd get in there and they'd find my grandfather was sitting in it! ... always wondered how he got there!"
Jack Buck

"I started in an office, in a shoeshop called Russell's down in St. Mary's for a few months, but I found it very difficult after school hours from nine to seven in an office with older people and my uncle was a chief

Shirley Road, with the Atherley on the right, about 1937.

operator at the Atherley, he said there was a job going and would I like it, of course I jumped at it, I was fourteen, I was an usherette."
Dorothy McAllen

"We all went to the Atherley cinema and, during the course of the programme, the lights came on and they said 'An air raid warning has been sounded, anyone who wishes to leave may do so in a quiet and orderly manner'. Then the lights went back down again. Well, we still sat there and after a time - I'm not sure how long, a gentleman in a dress suit - all the cinema managers wore dress suits in those days and bow ties - came down and spoke to my husband and his friend because they were both in Army uniform. My husband said 'I won't be long' and disappeared. I found out later they had been on the roof putting out incendiary bombs with sandbags. Well, as we came out of the cinema, the whole of the gutter around the Atherley cinema was ringed with incendiary bombs. Thank goodness they all fell in the gutter."
Betty Hooper

"One thing about the Atherley is although they turned it into a Bingo hall they kept the original front doors... and inside they've still got the little alcoves, like boxes at the back, you could go in there and be covered in, my mum has taken us in there when she was breastfeeding and fed (the baby) in there."
Pamela Humphrey

REGENT
"The Shirley Bully"

The original Cinema Hall, Park Street, Shirley. Private Collection.

There were successively two cinemas in Park Street, Shirley - the first demolished to make way for the second.

The original Cinema Hall opened in December 1913 with a film called *Her Supreme Sacrifice*. The building, probably a conversion, with the addition of projection box, entrance canopy and hoardings, contained an auditorium measuring 53 by 37 ft., with about 500 seats.

By November 1914 the Cinema Hall was styling itself the Regent Cinema. An advertisement that month named Mr. W. P. Christmas as proprietor and J. Lewis as manager. They evidently sought to undercut their rivals for prices were then only 2d., 3d., and 4d., in the evenings and 1d., 2d., and 3d., for the children's Saturday matinees - to which boys from the local Seamen's Orphanage were invited as the manager's guests. There were normally two houses within the 6.00 to 10.30 p.m. evening session but on 18th December 1914 the Regent screened one long "Grand Benefit Performance" from 6.45 to 10.30 p.m., for the Mayor's Distress Relief Fund.

By 1925 seat prices ranged from 6d., to 1s., and ten years later they were still only 6d., to 1s. 3d. - excellent value, because by then the original Regent had closed in 1929 and been replaced by a new "super cinema", then owned by Messrs. Palmer and Clement. This opened on Bank Holiday Monday, 1st August 1932, when the first films were *The Dove*, starring Dolores del Rio, and *Ladies of the Jury*, with Edna May Oliver.

This 1,300 seat cinema had stalls and a balcony with entrances in Park Street and Shirley High Street, the High Street entrance having originally been a shop. The cinema was well advertised with signs on the front and side of the building and a glass canopy to shelter patrons while queuing.

Irene Taylor (on right). Projectionist at the Regent in the 1950's. Private Collection.

Programmes were mostly second-run films, with a serial also shown each week. There was a well run children's Saturday picture show and the Southampton Film Society held meetings there for fifteen years. When the Regent had an orchestra one of Southampton's well known band leaders, Gil Hume, played violin here.

In 1945 the Regent became one of George Wright's chain but falling audiences eventually saw planning permission granted to change the building to shops and flats. It closed on 9th September 1961 with a Disney film *The Absent Minded Professor*, starring Fred MacMurray, and subsequently was replaced by a supermarket.

"We had the Regent .. up where Sainsbury's is now, in fact you can still see the name Regent faintly on the wall over Contessa; that was unique you know, you could go in that way and you could go in the side entrance by Sainsbury's. The cheaper seats on the side, the shillings as we called it, you would get all the

DREAM PALACES

Shirley High Street entrance. The film showing c.1960 was Swiss Family Robinson with John Mills and Dorothy McGuire.

kids down there and it had a partition across. In the interval we used to hop over and the old commissionaire used to drag us back.... If you wanted to pay for the circle or the upper stalls you would go in Shirley High Street way and it was very plush in there"
Pamela Humphrey

"Later my Aunt played at the Regent Cinema and it was, at this time, when my Mother used to take me to the Regent, that I used to listen intently to 'Gil Hulme' playing the violin with my Aunt. I loved the violin from my very early years. During the time my Aunt was at the Regent several violinists came and then moved on. At one time there was young Molly Hampton, who was to be a friend of all of us. I used to call her 'Auntie Molly'. She later played at the 'Lyric', Cobden Bridge. Others who followed were Peggy Irvine, Mr. Yendell and Mrs. Williams. Doorman was Mr. Hooper. He got the name 'The Shirley Bully'. He certainly kept order during performances. Anyone not behaving he would promptly eject."
Eddie Dawe

"In 1950 I read in the paper, second projectionist wanted at the Regent cinema in Shirley, so I thought right, that's me, I'm going to try... I was taken on there for a trial and there were two more boys there and a re-wind boy and a Chief. I was going to be the second so I had no problem with being a woman, we didn't seem to have those problems then, I don't know why...

...The Regent... it was quite a nice cinema and we used to have the second run films, we didn't get many Rank because we were registered to the MGM, that means it goes to the Forum or the Empire which is now the Mayflower it'd go to those cinemas first and then it'd come to us, second run...

...People used to smoke a lot then and the screen, used to get dark. Now the screen is not just a plain white thing it's like a rubberised, perforated, and it's stretched on iron frames. One day the general manager, Mr. Cox he said 'right', washable paint had only just come in then, 'right well we'll do that screen over with emulsion paint'; course, it looked beautiful, we had a beautiful brilliant picture, but the sound

The Regent entrance in the 1960's

was all muffled, being washing paint it'd gone into all the speakers and it nearly clogged the holes up through the perforations, It had filled all these holes up, so it was funny really to see the two boys, down on their knees, pricking all these little holes out, where the speakers were...

...Oh, Mario Lanza, Mario Lanza (in The Great Caruso) I remember, it had been to the Forum and then it came to us and on the last night of the showing we had so many people outside when we started the last house that the manager said to them 'well if you don't mind waiting', so we carried on that morning till two o'clock, till everybody had seen the whole film through...

...At the Regent, we were the only cinema that could carry on when there was a power cut, because we used to generate our own electricity, we were the only cinema in Southampton that could do that."
Irene Taylor

"I happened to see a job advertised in the Echo for a trainee projectionist at the Regent Cinema in Shirley, I went straight up there and got the job, that was in 1957 and I was there until it closed down in 1962. I was sixteen when I got the job. When I worked in the Regent on my night off I used to go to the pictures. My training was mostly how to operate cameras, general work, winding back film, cleaning the stage, believe it or not you had to clean the screen, get a big brush and wipe all the dust off."
John Harris

THE RIALTO
"Part and parcel of cinema"

The Rialto building, for sale after the cinema closed in 1960.

This 928 seat purpose built cinema at 325 Shirley Road, on the corner with Janson Road, opened on 9th January 1922. The opening ceremony before an invited audience was performed by the actress Stella Muir - who starred in *The Heart of a Rose* the highlight of the first programme. An orchestra accompanied the silent film.

The Rialto had a coloured tiled front, with a long foyer leading to the auditorium and a balcony above. The side wall along Janson Road still shows the cinema name in clear lettering. The original owner was Mr. Joe Rose. He was followed by other 'independents' until Oscar Deutsch bought the Rialto for the Odeon circuit in 1937; it was later absorbed into the Rank Organisation.

At the time of its closure on 5th November 1960, the staff comprised the manager, Mr. Tommy Smith, four projectionists, two doormen, six usherettes and four cleaners. The last film was Mike Todd's *Around the World in Eighty Days*. After being stripped of its cinema fittings the building was used as a warehouse and the foyer as a showroom. Its painted frontage still resembles a cinema.

"The Standard in East Street was known as the bug hutch but the Kings Theatre in Kingsland Square that was great, I actually saw silent films there, I saw silent films at the Rialto too, my Dad took me to the silent film of Tom Sawyer, must have been very young but I can remember it quite well."
Sam Cooper

"The Rialto ... there was a private box on the left hand side of the circle; it was mainly used on a Sunday night when the cinema was very very busy... after sweeping the place out every morning we used to use an enlarged type of flit gun like a gardener would use on his roses but this had scented disinfectant in it and we used to give the auditorium a good liberal sprinkling of the stuff to sweeten it up. The only time the Rialto got any fresh air was when I opened the side doors into Janson Road, while I was

sweeping the place out. I remember on one occasion in the circle I gave one of the seats a thump with a broom handle and a whacking great cloud of dust arrived, I don't think they'd been cleaned since 1921 when they were put in."

Bert Mayell

"When I was between the age of twelve to fourteen years, I used to go to the Rialto; my big interest was the orchestra. I think there was about six in the orchestra, which was under the direction of Mr. Austen Rigby. The lead violinist was 'Tommy Groves'. I also remember well Mr. Hill, the commissionaire, who used to come down during the interval and play the drums."

Eddie Dawe

"While I was there it had separate gas radiators, the boiler wasn't connected to any heating system, the place actually had gas radiators, about four down each side of the auditorium and three across in front of the stage and you'd see the little red glow of each through the side glass that they were still alight and if one blew out I used to go to the taper and light it up, in among the audience, you know; that's just part and parcel of cinema."

Bert Mayell

"When you got to a certain age, like twelve or thirteen, you were given responsibility then because you used to go every week and you were a permanent member and we performed the traffic control outside. It was the Odeon National Cinema Club for boys and girls, it was in all cinemas. I think the Rialto was an Odeon cinema, the Atherley wasn't, they didn't actually have a club, they just had Saturday morning pictures..."

Pamela Humphrey

Children's Saturday Pictures

The ABC Minors song sung at the start of the show was:

> We are the boys and girls
> Well known as minors of the ABC
> And every Saturday all line up to see
> The films we like and shout aloud with glee
> We like to laugh and have our sing song
> Just a happy crowd are we
> We're all pals together
> We're minors of the ABC

The Gaumont British Saturday Matinee song was:

> We come along on Saturday morning
> Greeting everybody with a smile
> We come along on Saturday morning
> Knowing it's well worth while
> As members of the G.B. club we all intend to be
> Good citizens when we grow up
> and champions of the free
> We come along Saturday morning
> Greeting everybody with a smile, smile, smile
> Greeting everybody with a smile.

Cards of the Odeon National Cinema Club for boys and girls, issued to Pamela Bowles at the Rialto in the early post war years. Private Collection.

BITTERNE
"Great fun for the kids"

Chapel Street. The building on the right was a cinema in the 1920's. Bitterne Local History Society.

The cinema was a conversion from a church or church hall at 75 Chapel Street and only operated for two years from 1924 to 1925. It was also known to some as Dean Road cinema following the change of name in 1924, to end confusing duplications after the 1920 extension of the borough boundary east of the Itchen.

The operator built a very small projection box on the front and after closure it was used by Smalls the Builders as a workshop. The building still stands, now very much altered to a private house.

"I must have been learning the violin for five or six years and when I was eighteen or nineteen played at the Bitterne Cinema in Chapel Street (now Dean Road) more or less for fun really ... ... I think I went there to see a film and asked if I could play there. The young lady who played the piano was the daughter of the owner and I used to read the music over her shoulder. All the children from Bitterne used to go there on a Saturday morning, it was great fun for the kids, cost 1d to go in or something like that...

...The piano was down in the front, an upright piano, there was a partition which might have been cloth, I stood there and played for one and a half to two hours for the children's' matinees."
Leslie Bradfield

Dean Road, Bitterne in 1974. The space for the projection box on the front is still visible. Bitterne Local History Society.

RITZ

"The building seemed to lift up and come down again"

Ritz Cinema c.1951. Patrons could enjoy a Cecil B. de Mille epic Samson and Delilah starring Victor Mature and Hedy Lamarr or the remake of Showboat with Howard Keel and Ava Gardner. Private Collection.

The Ritz in Bitterne Road opened its doors on 28th October 1936 with the film *Jack of All Trades*. There was no special ceremony. Built by Brazier and Son Ltd., the 800 seat cinema was thought to have a bright future in this part of town as a family-type cinema showing films with wide appeal. This was especially good for children as the cinema had a Saturday morning film show with admission at 6d. Up to 700 regularly attended. Among the patrons was Rosemary Rogers who would deliver the weekend meat to the manager from her father's butchers shop at the top of Lances Hill. She would stay to see the film at the invitation of the manager as long as her Dad had approved it as suitable.

The Ritz was taken over in 1957/58 by Harry Mears Theatres Ltd., who spent a lot of money refurbishing and re-equipping the interior but unfortunately this failed to attract enough patrons to keep it going. Among the staff was Mr. Arthur Smith, the doorman, who joined the cinema just after its opening. Its last manager was Mr. Paton who reflected that they tried all types of films to get a full audience but finally the Ritz closed on 1st July 1961 with *The Last Command*. The last Saturday morning show saw 600 children turn up, to be joined by Mr. Paton's Great Dane "Sandra", a great favourite of theirs. After closure, the cinema was demolished and shops and a bowling alley built on the site.

"At the Ritz we had a doorman, a commissionaire and a pageboy, and usually the pageboys would graduate up to the projection room, I was never a pageboy...

...The headmaster came to me one day and said there's this vacancy going at the Ritz and he knew the circumstances ... it was a bit of a struggle, and in those days, my wages were the best of any industry, they were highly paid for those days, you know we're talking about '36, '37 and I started, as I say, with my bike, taking the newsreel from the Ritz at Bitterne to Woolston and from Woolston back to Bitterne, for each programme, and I used to get twelve and six, and half a crown for my bike, fifteen bob a week, in those days there were many, many, men who weren't earning that."

John Fanstone

"*Called the Ritz, but I completely forget what the picture was. I know it was quite an interesting one, by that time of course, things were getting more and more hectic and it was quite a treat to go to the cinema anyway. But during the performance... we were conscious of the fact that something was happening although there hadn't been an alarm given. There was a few ominous noises and eventually the manager made an announcement that the film would be stopped for a short period, when anybody who wished to could leave the cinema as there was an air raid in progress. So they cut the film for a few minutes. I said to my wife, 'what we going to do?' 'We'll stay', we'd got interested in the film. We stayed, but gradually the noises began to get more and more ominous until eventually there was a tremendous crunch and the building seemed to lift up and come down again. We decided it perhaps was time to go then! So we left, well actually I'd played football that afternoon, one of the few games one had managed to get around that time, and had my bicycle with me, so my wife sat on the bar and off we pedalled to get from Bitterne to Sholing, but on at least three occasions on that journey we dropped the bike and dived for the nearest wall.*"

Jimmy Mead

Advertising leaflet for children - with additional tips on road safety and keeping dry. Private Collection.

WOOLSTON PICTURE HOUSE
"Left in mid-air with the train going over the cliff!"

The interior of the Woolston Cinema during 'silent' days. Private Collection.

The Woolston Picture House followed the Atherley as Southampton's second purpose-built cinema - although Woolston was not actually incorporated into the borough until 1920. The Woolston cinema opened in 1913, offering some 600 seats at 3d., 6d., and 1s. for continuous performances running from 2.00 to 10.30 p.m. It appealed strongly as a neighbourhood and family cinema, drawing good houses and remaining in business for sixty years.

Taking advantage of the location in Portsmouth Road, the name of the cinema was painted on the roof, where it was visible to passengers crossing the river Itchen on the floating bridges. The frontage had a collection of heads in roundels painted on the upper part of the facade resembling Shakespeare, Bacon, Britannia and other historical figures. The cinema also served as the venue for many meetings of workers from the nearby Thornycroft shipyard.

The cinema had many owners including Harry Mears who bought it in 1957, when the stage area was altered for the installation of a Cinemascope screen. This also involved the front seats being removed and the rest of the seating reorganised. The last film shown was Disney's *The Worlds Greatest Athlete* on 1st September 1973. Since then the building has been used as a bingo hall, but still retains many of its features as a cinema, particularly its frontage.

Unemployment demonstration outside the cinema. c.1930.

DREAM PALACES

"True cinema starts as a child, its your first cinema; now the first one I worked in was the Rialto but the first one I remember going in was Woolston and to me Woolston is the home of cinema, that's where all my dreams were nurtured; I've met the outside world through the front two rows in Woolston, fivepence a go and I wouldn't have changed it"

Bert Mayell

The Cinema Shop. Private Collection

"We used to go up the road and tear a paper ticket off the advertisement in Frampton's cold meat shop and then go and pass it over to get the proper tickets and then we used to steal more tickets, the metal ones to hand over to our mates who were waiting in the toilet for us... ...Another way in at the back, go up into Oakbank Road and go up the back cut between Langthorn's paper shop and Palmer's cycle shop and open up the back, someone inside would open up the little fire escape door at the back and let the boys in that way...

...Well, in the silent days, oh, there was nearly always the serial, that left you in mid-air with the train going off the top of the cliff, continued next week, they'd get you to come back the following week.

William Ryan

"So I left school in March and my idea was to work in a cinema, nothing else existed, you could be an errand boy, you could work at Thornycroft's yard or down in one of the aircraft factories, or whatever, but I was interested in cinema and I used to go as often as I could, as I said earlier, money was in short supply really but my Dad always found one and six for myself and my two brothers to go to the pictures, on Saturday mainly, and it was fivepence in the Woolston and a penny to spend, well this was riches

indeed and I was fascinated. Woolston, as you know, has like a very short foyer, the depth was about six feet and right behind there was a grand sort of projection room... and they used to have the doors open and you could peep in and I used to pray they'd got the doors open that I could peep in... and you could hear them (projectors) ticking away, ... I used to spend a lot of time looking around, not to disturb people but to see that beam coming through the porthole and blue white light expanding the size of the screen and dancing away like the devil on horse racing or motor racing and things like that. Absolutely captivated, so I had to work in the cinema".

Bert Mayell

Charlie Asplin, roller skating Manager of the cinema in the 1930's.

"The manager was named Charlie Asplin and he was very much facially like the great film star Adolphe Menjou, waxen moustache, always a smart suit, gold watch and chain and never had anything on the end, it was just a chain, no watch no medals or anything; it was just a chain hung across his chest to make it look like important."

William Ryan

The interior with the new Cinemascope screen in the 1960's. Private Collection.

"...at Woolston yes we did have double seats at the back, and up in the circle and they used to get broken more than what the single ones did... ...it was one of the oldest cinemas, it was built as a cinema in 1912. It was very very ornate, the ceiling had huge arches going right across, looked as if it was supporting it but it wasn't, it was decor, it was plaster, it was excellent, all mouldings and marvellous, they took lorry loads and lorry loads away when they refurbished in '57. There was two big pillars down the front, that supported a lion on each, and when they were pulled down, one of the lions was given to one of the cleaners, she wanted it for her garden, it was huge, as big as me, only longways!"

John Fanstone

Edgar Dawe, doorman at the Woolston Cinema.

OTHER CINEMAS IN THE LOCALITY
"The air raid warning has sounded"

Neighbouring towns and villages all had their own local cinemas, which could be reached by bus from Southampton. Romsey had three cinemas - The Elite, Corn Exchange and the Ritz. There were two at Eastleigh - the Picture House, which opened in 1932 and closed in 1959 and the Regal, the latter opened in 1928 in a former variety theatre; it was modernised and reconstructed in 1936 and continued in operation until it finally closed in 1980, to become a night-club.

Totton cinemas were the Electric Theatre and the Savoy, opened in 1935 and closed in 1961. At Lyndhurst there was the Plaza while New Milton had its Waverley which closed in 1972. The Hampton cinema at Hythe opened in 1923 and ran for 40 years, while the Esso at Holbury still operates. Another Waterside cinema not to be forgotten was the 400 seater for the RAF at Calshot.

Abbey

The Abbey Cinema at Victoria Road, Netley, opened for business on 11th April 1938. The opening films were *King Solomon's Mines* and *Oh Doctor!* Surviving the Blitz, the Abbey continued to show films until its closure in October 1958. Today the distinctive building is a second hand furniture shop but even among the assorted beds, tables and desks a strong sense of the cinema persists. Bert Mayell was working as a rewind boy at the Rialto in Shirley when he heard that the Abbey was being built in Netley. Keen to get on and work closer to home he secured the position of third projectionist.

"I agonised for days, trying to pluck up courage to give my notice, so eventually I told the Chief, I said look Alf, there's a new cinema opening at Netley ... so anyway, on the following Monday, off to Netley I went, there it was a brand new little cinema, lovely, no problem at all, so I went up to the projection room, lovely parquet floor, no sweeping to do, that was it, I'd now grown up. Only one snag, when you sweep out a cinema, the perks are yours and you can find a couple of coppers, penny tuppence, or threepence, sometimes a shilling! ... ... About a fortnight after we opened we were showing a little Metro Goldwyn Mayer film, one of the crime does not pay series, where after the logo there's a revolver facing the audience and the man pulls the trigger three or four times. Well when he shot this gun the explosion hit the back wall of the cinema, bounced all round the place, it sounded like a machine gun, the acoustics were wrong so something had to be done and fast... they had to deaden the back wall, so the following day the back wall was battened, all patch tiles, acoustic tiles were fitted and the problem solved, in absolutely no time flat and it was a little four hundred seater, and it was perfect... ...at the Abbey, we had the manager, cashier, ice cream girl, four usherettes and three projectionists... Sunday night was the best night, you had a separate programme and I think that's when they recovered all their costs, on a Sunday, that paid for the rest of the week, because even in the heyday of cinemas, matinees were pretty empty, you didn't get many people at matinees...

Bert Mayell, Cinema Projectionist at the Abbey, Netley and the Rialto Shirley, 1940. Private Collection

...We had a slide machine and when an air-raid warning went we put a slide on the screen to say the air raid warning's sounded, patrons wishing to leave may do so by any exit but the show will continue, so under this glass roof we carried on showing the films. Now at Woolston they couldn't do that because at Woolston they did not have a slide machine so whoever was in charge at the time, either the manager or relief manager or whatever, used to go down into the audience, the projectionist would turn the sound down a little bit and he'd say 'ladies and gentlemen the air raid warning has sounded, if you wish to leave you may do so, but the show will continue and I'll let you know when the all clear goes', and the show just carried on and then when the all clear went he went down and said 'right the all clear's gone' and bob's your uncle, that was the system of warning...

...The servicemen used to arrive from the gun batteries or places like that and a lot of them used to bring their rifles with them and so these were taken from them and stored in a little room by the side of the manager's office, locked in there until the end of the performance and we'd unlock the door and then the NCO in charge of the detachment he would just dole out the rifles."

Bert Mayell

Bert Mayell in the Abbey cinema building in Netley. 1996. Today it is used as a second hand furniture store.

ON THE LINERS
"Watching the film backwards"

The cinema for Tourist class passengers on the second Mauretania in the late 1930's depicted on a C. R. Hoffman postcard. Private Collection.

For much of this century the port of Southampton has been synonymous with "floating palaces" and "ocean greyhounds", the great liners which crossed the world's oceans, especially the Atlantic. Between and after the wars, merging into the present era of cruise ships, they vied with each other to offer increasingly stylish and spacious public rooms and facilities, including ballrooms, swimming pools and cinemas. Films were a popular entertainment afloat, with big liners often providing two or three separate cinemas, to cater for the various classes of passengers (first, second and third/tourist) - reflecting the hierarchies of life aboard for them as well as the crews. Liner's crews were largely recruited from the Southampton area.

"Oh yes, I worked to nine or ten o'clock at night. Except when I was going to go to the movies, when I could. It was a bad ship for amusements (Queen Mary). The females - we had no place for when we were off duty. If we went to the cinema we went to the passengers', the Tourist class cinema, but we had to see the films backwards. Even if the place was empty we weren't allowed to see the film frontwards, in the chairs, we had to sit on the floor behind the screen. We had a master-at-arms one day and there were only two passengers and the passengers said, 'Why are the girls sitting behind there?' They said, 'Let the girls come here. There are only two of us.' But we weren't allowed to."

Marie Semple

The First Class Cinema on the Queen Elizabeth - another Hoffman postcard picture. Private Collection.

"When you were off-duty the cinema was open so, with the chief telephonist's permission, you could go and see a film. If you should go on duty at three o'clock, sometimes she would allow us to go to the cinema and we would come on at four o'clock. Then it would work, that they would go to the cinema and we would do vice-versa. But it was according to how the day was going whether you went or not. We were allowed to sit... we had to wait until all the passengers were in and they'd got where they wanted and we could sit in, you know, quite comfortable where we wanted to sit."
Edith Smith

Stena Line passengers enjoy a film en route to/from France. c.1995. Stena Line.

Cinema on board Queen Mary. Ocean Pictures.

CINEMAS IN SOUTHAMPTON DURING WORLD WAR TWO
"We never close"

In 1940 all hell was let loose, when I think back now telephonists and all sorts of people getting the O.B.E. etc., for sticking to their posts, all the cinemas throughout Britain and those projectionists with no steel helmets all up in those little rooms through the entire blitzes in Liverpool, London and the films always went on until maybe the place caught alight."
John Cooper

New cinemas were being built right up to the end of the Thirties but construction came to an end with the outbreak of war. At the beginning of the war, as a safety precaution, cinemas were closed but, with no immediate bombing, soon reopened with larger audiences than ever. Throughout the war people continued to visit the cinema. On one hand the cinema provided an escape from the harsh realities of life in wartime Britain while on the other it provided an opportunity through newsreels to get the latest news from the war zones where many had relatives and friends serving with the forces. In the early part of the war when invasion by Germany seemed a real possibility, newsreels of refugees fleeing across Europe and the retreat from Dunkirk had a profound effect.

"They had shops at the Bargate, temporary shops at the Bargate and on her day off (my mother) used to take me to the Cinema with her. Now this led me to seeing some weird weepy women's films and a very scary version of Phantom of the Opera with Claud Rains, which gave me nightmares for ages, but one of the things that made the biggest impact on me was that when she took me to the cinema I also saw the newsreels; now the thing that really influenced me more than anything was the newsreels which showed refugees. Refugees on the road in Europe, and I thought, come the invasion I'm going to be ready. So I used to go home after these newsreels and I never said anything to anyone... not until quite a few years ago, I used to go home and I had a dolls pram, very

At the height of the bombing raids many were made homeless and others left the town at night to sleep in the surrounding countryside. Imperial War Museum.

deep bodied in the fashion of the real prams at the time, with sort of pads across, halfway and I used to practice packing my pram for when I was going to be a refugee. I was quite serious, wildly impractical. I never thought of packing any clothes or any food, but the first thing that went in was my collection of 'Sunny' stories. I used to take out the little ledges on which the doll actually rested and I used to pack in all underneath. I mean mothers used to in those days. Take out the bottom ledge and put all their shopping in the base of the prams when they took the babies out. Well I used to do the same thing, I packed everything, all I considered essential for being a refugee into the bottom of my pram."
Barbara Burbridge

Southampton and its people experienced an eventful war. The first bombs fell in the borough on 19th June 1940 and the last recorded "all clear" went off at 8.08 p.m. on Sunday 5th November 1944. During this period 30,652 incendiary and 2,631 high explosive devices fell, killing 631 and injuring 1,888. Over 40,000 properties were damaged, 11,000 of which beyond repair. Cinemas and other places of entertainment did not escape unscathed.

On 26th September 1940 at 4.20 p.m. two waves of German planes swept in from the sea dropping more than 200 bombs over an area of a square mile; 55 people lost their lives. The central target was the Supermarine Aviation works at Woolston, home of the Spitfire. The factory received eight direct hits, killing several workers. Fortunately for long-term production much of the work of the factory had already been dispersed throughout the locality. On the day of the raid John Cooper was working in the Plaza Cinema in Northam Road, further up the River Itchen from the works.

"I was up outside the projection room one day, very high up on the roof and over my head came a couple of messerschmitts, I could see the pilots and they shot all the barrage balloons down, so I had a grandstand view of the whole town of flaming barrage balloons and literally the sirens didn't go until the raid had started and I looked down and there was a whole mass armada of aircraft coming up Southampton Water and the next thing of course you ducked, the whole place shook, Supermarine got blown to kingdom come and when I popped up again of course it was all a flaming wreck."
John Cooper

"I stood on the steps of the Regal cinema and I watched a German aircraft come in and shoot balloons down and then the bombers came in and started bombing Supermarine and you could literally stand there and watch the bombs coming down. It was a dreadful experience really and truly."
Ada Rogers

During October and November 1940 the raids on the town continued, eventually reaching a climax with a series of particularly heavy raids which took place during the night of Saturday 23rd November, and a week later, on the consecutive nights of 30th November and 1st December. It is these raids that have become known as "Southampton Blitz" with over 200 people killed and much of the town centre decimated.

Above Bar, looking north. The bombing raids are already devastating the town. c.1941.

"There were three particularly bad nights, the first Saturday night all I remember was the place shaking and putting my head out of the door and flames etc., and the next Saturday was the worst, I even remember the film I was showing, by that time I was third projectionist and I was showing Shirley Temple in the 'Bluebird' and the whole place was shuddering and shaking and I was left alone, but what I didn't know was the manager and the Chief Operator were putting out incendiaries. But I carried on and the projection was sometimes slightly off the screen and I would have to bash it back, then the emergency light would come on, some of the seats were on fire; an

incendiary had come through in front of the projection room and the manager was there with the Chief Projectionist putting water up and we then shut down."

John Cooper

Reeling from the raids, Sotonians emerged from their shelters to find their town altered beyond recognition. For centuries the point of departure for British armies bound for foreign shores, now the town was visited directly by war for the first time since the French raid of 1338. On 5th December 1940, four days after the Blitz, King George VI visited the stricken town. Crowds lined the streets around the Civic Centre and the various Civil Defence Services were inspected. Lawrence Burgess, for many years Deputy Librarian in Southampton, was serving as a Special Constable during the war and remembered the visit well.

Winston Churchill inspecting Civil Defence Forces outside the Civic Centre 31st January 1941.

"On the day of this story I was doing some lunch-break shopping in Above Bar when I was pulled up by an unusual sight. Instead of the normal queue making advance booking at the Forum there was a rope in place to prevent a queue from forming. As I looked, suddenly a stranger clapped his hand on my shoulder. I wheeled round sharply - and presto! It was no stranger but the boy who occupied the desk next to mine at school in Kingston - some thirty years previously. After some irrelevant chat he informed me that he was now Chief Consultant Engineer for ABC and he was here in Southampton on account of the trouble that had closed the booking queue.

The previous evening had been fairly normal: Jerry chuntering overhead and the usual ack ack greeting.

Or was that all? Inside the Forum things were normal until a sudden jolt shook the whole building. The management took no chances, the projector stopped; after a cautionary explanation the house was cleared and the staff divided into small teams to inspect all the premises.

The inspection was quick and efficient: nothing to report. The last two doorkeepers stood in the entrance. When the first man produced his keys his mate called out 'Just a minute, I'm popping into the Gents.' He swung open the door and behold, no Gents! From roof to basement there was one big pit; above him the stairs and below ... well, a very nasty looking job - still unexploded too. In fact, one of the biggest bombs so far received. I gathered that my friend had hurried over post haste and the bomb disposal boys were expected.

Well, while we were talking, time had been running out so I took the short cut to West Marlands Road. Thus I confronted, within about fifty yards, a dais with all the trimmings of a saluting stand. I suddenly remembered that the various voluntary services were due to be inspected by the King that very afternoon. 'Well', I thought, 'that's out of the question now.'

I reached my office and got on with some work, but soon I was worried by great crowds lining the streets, waving flags and doing all the other daft things crowds do. Eventually the King's party arrived and the long procession started to file past. Thud, thud, thud went the boots; Blah, blah, blah went the bands and presumably all the little fuses were trembling with excitement. The whole business was a great success. The King told them they were a fine body of men and how pleased he was with them, then he left to catch his train.

Within a few minutes of the Royal Train leaving the station, every person in the centre of the City (not just the Civic Centre) was compelled to get right out of the central zone. I remember I was not given time to collect my coat. The bomb disposal boys did their stuff yet again and all was well.

When the Echo commemorated the present Queen's Coronation they issued an impressive little booklet about Southampton's relations with the Royal Family.

We think of the Echo staff as a nest of singing birds, but, surprisingly, though they provided the pictures, the whole of the text was written by me. I could not resist the temptation: my fervent eulogy of George VI praised him warmly for the personal risks he ran while encouraging his devoted subjects in this City. The joke was that only one man in the Civic Centre knew what I was talking about - Mr. Freeman, then Education Secretary: we had quite a chuckle about it.

It is rather curious that since those far-off days quite a number of speakers and writers have chosen to quote some of my more purple passages - especially this one about George VI. No one has so far seen the point. I'm no fanatical Royalist, but just consider the danger deliberately incurred for the King and some thousands of others rather than make a few telephone calls... well, I was appalled! I have never tried to find out who the exalted idiot was: I shouldn't be safe in possession of that knowledge. If he's already passed over, perhaps he's jot a job watching the gates of hell, as I used to watch over unexploded bombs. Every 'Hosannah' shakes a fuse. R.I.P."

L. A. Burgess (from Southampton at War 1939 - 1945)

Immediately after the blitz all the town's cinemas closed as normal life ground to a halt. Several cinemas and theatres as well as the Forum were destroyed or damaged by the bombing and subsequent fires. The Picture House was completely gutted by fire. The then newest cinema in the town, Cinenews suffered fire damage to its foyer and entrance. The Gaiety escaped with just five incendiaries on the roof, four burning themselves out and the small fire created by the other extinguished by the manager Mr. Davies, who was also a warden. The Gaiety was the only cinema to have its own basement shelter. The Lyric, Kings and Standard would never re-open for business.

Of the theatres, the Palace in the High Street was destroyed. The New Hippodrome (Grand) had bombs in the stage and dressing room area but the auditorium remained undamaged.

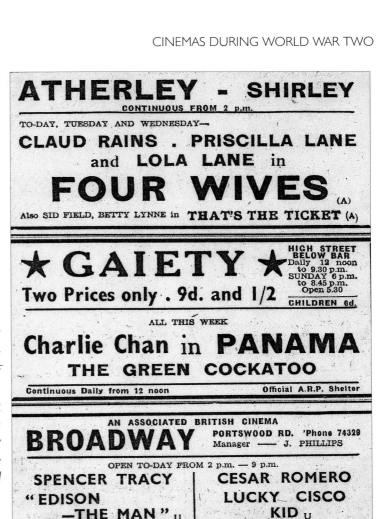

Only one week after the "Blitz" the neighbourhood cinemas offer a full programme. 9th December 1940. Southern Daily Echo.

In the suburbs the Palladium at Portswood was used as a casualty station for people injured during a raid. Staff assisted helping the injured. By 6th December 1940 five cinemas were able to re-open for business, namely the Savoy, Atherley, Broadway, Palladium and the Ritz at Bitterne.

Wherever possible during the war cinemas adopted a policy of "we never close", made famous by the Windmill Theatre in London. During films messages were displayed by slide onto the screen warning the audience of an impending raid, at which point they could leave, collecting a refund on their way. On many occasions few people left and continued watching the film with raids going on around them. In fact the cinema was often as good a place as any to be in a raid, with heavy steel work, strong side walls and occasionally a reinforced concrete roof. In particularly bad raids audiences were advised to use nearby public shelters.

Nationally, the actual number of cinema buildings destroyed was relatively small, given that there were between five and six thousand open at the

Mrs Katherine Bates pictured at work as a cinema projectionist. 1941. Southern Daily Echo.

beginning of the war. For example, of three hundred Odeon cinemas only one was destroyed and that was situated in a City centre. Most suburban cinemas escaped major damage and, as in Southampton, continued to show films when City centre ones were closed.

During the early years of the war several Mass Observation investigators were sent to Southampton. They were employed by the Home Intelligence Department of the Ministry of Information to be present in towns undergoing enemy bombardment and to report conditions and morale. In early 1941, when Southampton was still the subject of regular raids, one investigator looked at the availability of restaurants and places of entertainment in the town centre. On 20th February 1941 he found the Regal Cinema Cafe "full mainly 'C' class, enjoying a two shilling lunch with no meat after 1.00 p.m. only fish". He also reported for "those people who stay in the town at night, entertainment is therefore limited to local cinemas and pubs, and for the younger people and Forces, dancing nightly at the Banister Hall and weekly or bi-weekly at the Guildhall."

Special film shows were arranged for service personnel and often groups of sailors, on shore leave from their ships berthed in the docks, could be seen queuing outside cinemas . Licences were sought to show films on a Sunday and approval was usually limited to certain times such as 4.30 to 10.30 p.m. Another solution was two complete showings with some of the profits donated to charity.

Ministry of Information films charting the progress of the war supplemented newsreels. The Ministry also funded vans with back projection screens to tour localities showing films relating to air-raid precautions, war time cooking and other areas of self help.

Weekly returns for the Regal in 1943 show Sunday closely following Saturday as the most popular day to visit the cinema. During the week ending 26th June 1943, 15,029 people attended, an increase of almost 5,000 on the year before. The films shown that week were *Immortal Sergeant* supported by *Harvest Days* with the Manager G. Birke reporting "The feature was much enjoyed and well commented upon. The war theme, together with the brilliant weather, kept down receipts. The support was classed as being very poor." He also noted under "Sunday Thoughts" that "There appeared to be no reaction on the part of our patrons", presumably to this new opportunity to go to the cinema on the Sabbath. During that week also you could have seen *A Night to Remember* and *Blackie goes to Hollywood* at the

Empire, *Three Hearts for Julia* and *Flight Lieutenant* at the Forum or *Moon over Miami* and *Dive Bomber* at the Classic. A month later in July the unsigned Regal return bemoans "an excellent week's programme (*Shadow of a Doubt*) but I'm afraid the 'Stay at Home Holiday' programme arranged by the Borough Council has affected our receipts".

Also in July 1943 the United States Army 14th Major Transportation Corps arrived in the town. Initially their headquarters were in the Maritime Chambers in the old docks, but they later moved to the Civic Centre. They also had a headquarters in Hoglands Park. Members of the Corps were to be involved in the transportation of troops, supplies and prisoners of war to and from France over the next three years. In this period three and a half million British, American, Canadian and other troops passed through the town. For many of the American troops a visit to the cinema was as close to home leave as they were likely to get, with so many films based and made in the United States. During the period around the D-Day landings, special continuous film shows were staged for troops based in and around the town.

Douglas Fairbanks Junior at Hillfield Sick Bay, Southampton, 2nd World War. S.A.S.

POST WAR DEVELOPMENTS

With the ending of the war and families becoming re-united, the need for public entertainment diminished. Cinema attendances dropped dramatically after the surge of the Forties and small privately owned cinemas became the first to close. Rising costs, strong competition from the national chains and falling attendances started the decline that soon became the mass closures of the 1950's and 1960's.

The introduction of new technological innovations like "Cinemascope", "Cinerama" and 70mm film, held the patron's attention, but at a cost to the film industry. "Cinemascope" was nick-named "letterbox", the picture on the screen being roughly two and a half times as wide as it was high. This needed a very large, wide screen. A cinema like the Plaza at Northam, with its wide proscenium, could accommodate the new screen without too much alteration. However, at cinemas like the Woolston with a smaller screen in a slight alcove, the screen was brought forward and the front rows of seats removed, to improve the sight lines.

No Southampton cinemas were altered to accommodate "Cinerama" as this needed a curved screen at least 75 feet wide and three projectors to throw the pictures on to the screen. However, a travelling production of How the West was Won came to town and the film was shown in a circus tent on a piece of land near the Post House Hotel.

The 70 mm film called "wide screen" was adopted in most large cinemas and all these new systems used "stereophonic" sound to create the illusion of people talking, for example, each side of the screen. Large speakers were placed at the back on each side and normally the whole of the cinema's sound system was upgraded. There were also films in 3D where the audience needed to wear glasses with red and green lens to enjoy the extra dimension whereby an object came out from the screen, whether a fighting fist, or a flaming arrow!

The main rival to the cinema was television, first shown before the war to a very limited audience, but much publicised at the Festival of Britain. When mass production provided an affordable set, the population deserted the cinema, sitting in their own homes to watch many of the features previously on offer at the pictures.

With the falling attendances, those cinemas that did not continue showing films or change over to bingo were made redundant and if not demolished were put to other uses, such as supermarkets, carpet warehouses, many types of shops, garages and even churches.

Many cinemas were too big and the major circuits came up with the idea of splitting the interior into two or three smaller screens, one with about 600 seats and the others seating 100 - 150 people. Both the Odeon and the Forum in Southampton were adapted internally to provide three separate screening areas. It would seem to be a short step to the multiplex, the first to open in Milton Keynes in 1955. This is one new building containing many cinemas, up to 12 or more, mostly built outside city centres with plenty of parking spaces and often near shopping malls or hypermarkets. The Cannon complex in Southampton, since renamed the MGM, opened in 1989. Planning permission is being sought to build another at Hedge End. This seems to be the pattern for cinemas of the future - until the next technical invention advancing the television or the video market. None of these forms of visual entertainment offer the atmosphere of sitting watching a film as part of a cinema audience.

CANNON / MGM MULTIPLEX
"Everything light and bright"

MGM. Multiplex

Southampton's latest commercial cinema was opened in Ocean Village on Friday 21st July 1989 after a Gala evening the night before. This is a five screen complex with a total seating of 1,650, each auditorium having a different number of seats. The larger one is used for the blockbuster films and the smaller ones for the specialist films which draw lesser audiences. The cost of construction was £3 million and each theatre is decorated to a high standard with comfortable seats affording good leg room. The screens surround a central foyer which houses the ticket booths and the sales stall and provides a comfortable area to wait for the films. All the latest films are shown here and it also operates a Saturday morning children's film show. Originally called the Cannon cinema, since September 1993 it is known as the MGM Multiplex.

"I think the advancement in the cinema today is really wonderful. When I first went into the one in Ocean Village I couldn't believe it when I walked in (projection room). I just couldn't believe it, in that one room there was five cinemas being served with five projectors, and you could hear a pin drop almost, with five projectors running, now in the old days, (with) one projector you had to shout to make yourself heard, for all the machinery, and there was five projectors running...."
John Fanstone

"I was amazed to find a huge open foyer, and access to several screen areas - everything was light and bright - and the way that the programme is arranged, where one can visit the cinema at different times makes it much easier than the old style fixed (times)...

...This is the cinema of today: maybe the Art Deco palaces of the 30's had more glamour and mystery - but going "to the movies" is now set up for people who value cinema not just for entertainment but as an easily accessible art form."
Jill Neale

DREAM PALACES

"I go to the cinema two or three times a month, usually the Multiplex in Ocean Village and sometimes the UCI cinema in Portsmouth, the screens are nice and big and there is a new sound system in the cinema which is very good, but the seats are uncomfortable...

... I like action films mainly, but also comedy, the last film I saw was 'Jumanji'; it was one of the best comedy films I've seen...

... the Odeon was my favourite cinema because of the size of the main screen and the fact that it was at a steep angle, the atmosphere was really nice, very lively...

... it costs about £7 or £8 to go to the cinema if I buy food, I can only afford it because I work in Pizza Hut, actually the cinema is where a lot of my money goes...

... I usually finish work at eleven at the week-ends and I go to the midnight shows...

... the first film I ever saw was 'The Return of the Jedi', with my parents when I was five, at the Odeon...

... I usually go with friends, I would be too embarrassed to go on my own, especially if someone I knew saw me."

David Meech.

Foyer of the M.G.M. Multiplex just before the evening rush 1996.

HARBOUR LIGHTS CINEMA
"A new kind of cinema"

Harbour Lights Cinema, Ocean Village 1996.

In March 1994 work started on this regional cinema at Ocean Village. It cost £1.3 million, funded by the City Council together with grants from the British Film Institute and Southern Arts. It was designed by architects, Burrel, Foley, Fischer to provide two auditoria, one seating 325 and the other 141. The building's strongly nautical lines reflect the shape of ocean liners which once filled the port and its glass foyer gives views of the docks and Ocean Village. It has comfortable seating with good leg room. Many types of film are presented, with an emphasis on those not shown by the major film circuits. It opened on 24th February 1995 with *Muriel's Wedding*.

"I've been to Harbour Lights about four or five times and the thing that made me go is that it shows films that you wouldn't see in the ordinary cinema. I live within walking distance of Ocean Village and that's real handy too except its not very easy to walk to because there's no pedestrian crossing. The initial thing that got me there was they showed films that were unusual or old classics or special films that you just wouldn't see anywhere else, but the thing I really like about it is that it feels really kind of safe, I felt safer being there on my own ... I suppose because of the kind of films they show but also because of the way the building is, it's quite small and quite manageable and the staff are like, more plugged in than they are in the big cinemas, it's really comfortable to be there on your own. Old films like 'Lawrence of Arabia' and 'Gone with the Wind' that you really would want to see on the big screen, it's not the same on video."

Julie Browne

"Harbour Lights has three audiences; the student... much more willing to experiment, take a chance and a risk because they are regular cinema goers, they don't see it so much as a risk; people who only go to the cinema a few times a year want to come and feel sure that they're going to enjoy the film and it isn't a

DREAM PALACES

risk. The dedicated film-goer will go and see films, foreign language films, classic films that have been re-released, they are interested in finding out ... the third group are cinema-goers, maybe they go to the MGM a lot and they see that Harbour Lights isn't for them, they think that Harbour Lights is about specialised films, off the wall films. That is the group of people I really want to get in here, I want to show them that cinema is really exciting and films which are so called off the wall films are not off the wall at all...

...'Blue Juice' is a surfing film based in Cornwall, it bombed everywhere in the country, absolutely failed; we had it on for three days and they were queuing round the block for it, we brought it back in the beginning of January and we're selling out, we've taken more in just a few screenings than practically any other cinema in the country and...'Carry on Screaming' when we showed it we thought maybe we'll get fifty or sixty people along, we had about 180 people in to see this old movie and it was a terrible print, but everybody seemed to really enjoy it, those are two things that stick in my mind as kind of strange."

Rod Varley

Barbara Windsor outside Harbour Lights launching the Comedy Film Festival 1996.

Jane Goldman and Jonathan Ross. Harbour Lights, Nov. 4 1995.

GANTRY
"Popular, cult, foreign and arthouse"

An audience at the Gantry about to enjoy a film presentation. 1990's. Gantry.

Originally a drill hall, to the rear of the Mayflower, the Gantry opened as a multi-arts venue in 1987.

Since 1990 it has provided a popular, cult, foreign and arthouse film programme with themes such as Asian film on Sunday afternoons and a new Chinese cinema series entitled "Made in Hong Kong."

A regular venue for the Southampton Film Festival, it has also staged practical workshops on film making, new media, the internet and computer art films.

"It was part of the film festival, we went to see the Creature from the Black Lagoon in 3D. We all had to wear special glasses, it was the first time my kids had experienced anything like it, it was great. The funniest thing was we were sitting at the front and when we turned round there was a sea of people all wearing identical ridiculous green and red specs."
Marilyn Michalowicz

"The Gantry is a great place to see films. But movies over two hours can take their toll because the seats are a bit hard. But thats more than made up for by the well stocked bar and the fact that you can have a drink while you're viewing."
Clare Wilson

The Gantry 1996.

SOUTHAMPTON'S FAMOUS FILM DIRECTOR

Film Director Ken Russell, was born in Southampton on the 3rd July 1927, 'the year talkies were born'. He grew up at 31 Belmont Road, Portswood, son of a shop owner who many older Sotonians still associate with 'Russell's Cheques'.

During his childhood he spent a great deal of time in Southampton Cinemas and began staging his own film shows.

"Mother used to take me every day practically, she had nothing to do, she'd been a shop girl and time hung heavily on her hands, she had a maid and a semi-detached house, could afford it, Dad earned twenty quid a week, it was enough to live in style and then talkies were born, and she became a film fan over night. In the thirties we regularly went pretty well every day and either before or after went to a tea dance at one of the big stores...

...well the ones which mum and I used to go to were the Picture House, the Odeon, the Forum, the Gaiety and the Classic; all the ones in the High Street and occasionally at the Broadway at Portswood, but I used to go there by myself more or less and the Palladium, she used to like going into town...

...Oh the Broadway was marvellous decor, it was all medieval and it had painted murals on the walls of knights in armour rescuing damsels from castles, pretty impressive but rather dull. We used to have tea frequently in the mezzanine and that was done out in Tudor style, it was quite a grand place...

...I saw one there that terrified me, I ran out of the cinema and didn't stop running till I was over Cobden Bridge, that was Secret of the Loch a film about the Loch Ness monster. I ran so fast out, I had to come back and get my mackintosh. There was a toy diver when they cut to the model of the diver going over the boat, he went over the side of a dinghy and then they always pulled up a severed rope and a severed wind pipe and the final time we went down when this had happened three times and I knew we were going to see the monster and it seemed to be a huge goldfish bowl with some fish floating about in it and then round the corner of this what appeared to be a cracked flower pot, came a plucked chicken and that was one of the most horrifying things I've ever seen in my life, to this very day and that's when my hair stood on end and I stood up and walked stiffly out and then ran, ...I don't remember seeing any more horror films!...

...I'd had a pathescope projector my parents bought for me for Christmas at Currys, just at the Bargate. I had Felix the Cat and Snob Pollard films, and Charlie Chaplin and you know, I showed them over and over and then I discovered you could get extension arms. I went through the pathescope catalogue, Martin's the chemist,they were bombed out and he operated from a private house near Archers Road, I used to go along and there were all these piles of blue packages with spools of nine point five and I went through them all and gave picture shows in my father's garage in aid of the Spitfire Fund, with music. I had one record that had 'Greek Homage March' on one side and Arthur Bliss' March from 'Things to Come' on the other and I showed all the features like 'Seigfried and The Spy' by Frtiz Lang and 'Metropolis', of course I showed that over and over...

...Then I went away to school at Pangbourne Nautical College and then I did a brief trip at the end of the war to New Zealand and back, in a convoy, by then I'm in my teens. I'd become a fanatical cinema-goer, obviously during term time at Pangbourne we only saw 16 mm films like Bulldog Jack and things like that. Then in holidays I used to catch up on all the films I'd missed, the general releases and I'd cycle round Southampton, I'd see three a day until I'd caught up, you know, because I could go to the second and third release houses...

Ken Russell has gone on to become one of Britain's best known film directors and has sometimes been referred to as its 'most controversial'. His many films have included *Women in Love*, *The Devils*, *The Music Lovers*, *The Rainbow* and *Salomés Last Dance*.

INDIAN FILMS
"Used to take food with us, crisps or drink"

Indian Film Poster 1970's

Since the post-war establishment of large communities of South Asian origin in the city, a variety of venues have shown Asian films, particularly the many Hindi films emanating from 'Bollywood', the centre of the industry in Bombay. Cinemas such as the Classic, Atherley and ABC all put on Asian films, mainly on a Sunday or very late on Saturday evenings. In the mid 1970's a club was set up and showed films in St. Luke's Hall on the corner of Onslow Road and Cranbury Avenue.

During the 1980's the availability of affordable video recorders resulted in the demise of regular shows; several video shops specialising in Asian films supplied the demand in the City. More recently, the advent of Satellite and Cable television with dedicated Asian language channels has provided a further outlet for film directly into the home.

In the 1990's however, attempts are being made to bring back big screen Asian films, with both the Gantry and Harbour Lights including them in their programmes.

"... there used to be late night (Asian) films at the ABC, Above Bar, like twelve o'clock at night, and that was Saturday night which was really inconvenient hours for families to go..."

Interior St. Lukes Hall, Indian Film Club mid 1970's. Private collection.

...I used to watch a lot of videos. I used to do 8mm movies (at home) I used to play around with cameras and projectors. Then I got involved into the 35mm...

... There was a ship that was going to be scrapped called the Ocean Monarch in 1975, something like that, and we bought the projectors off that ... it was advertised in the Echo that they were selling their equipment...

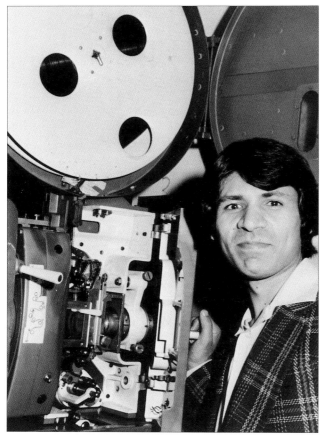

Nash Ladher in the projection room St. Lukes Hall. mid 1970's Private collection.

...We hired St. Luke's Hall and made some negotiations with the caretaker... we were going to use the stage side of it as a projection room and opposite we put a motorised screen and we used to pull the screen down and show the films there... ... we used to get the films from London, from Fangeet films... ... we used to show them over the weekend, there were a few people coming in seeing it plus this was a club, non profit making ... ... the seating capacity was only about one hundred and we used to get round about sixty people."
Nash Ladher

"On the corner of Onslow Road and Cranbury Avenue, they had the chairs lined one after the other and they had a portable screen and a projector, and it used to be quite busy. Sometimes there used to be about a hundred, sometimes there weren't any chairs so they'd stand at the back so that the women and the children sit on chairs and the men would stand at the back and watch it. On Saturday afternoons; we used to pay very little for them, around one pound, one pound fifty, depending on the film whether it was new or old, but most of the time they were very old films...

Left to right: Brininder Ladher, Jessy Ladher, Beljat Ladher, Micky Ladher, Jiggy Ladher, Dave Singh, Nash Ladher. Projection room at St. Lukes Hall is behind them. Dave and Nash ran the Film Club. Private collection.

...Yes, I used to take my children, they used to enjoy it ...used to take food with us, crisps and drinks, we did enjoy it, but in the end it had to close, because other cinemas started showing films."
Harbhajan

"...the first film I went to was in a cinema called ABC. ... and I was really shocked to see that many Asian people in Southampton because although it wasn't a very big cinema hall it was almost three quarters full and it was on a Sunday as well. The Indian film, the very first film I saw was 'Guide' that was the name of the film, a very popular film...

...Once those few cinema halls closed and the videos came out in the 1980's people have gone quite crazy watching Asian films, but now with the new Asian TV channel I would think 90% of them have it."
Kirpal Vedwan

FILM SOCIETIES AND OTHER VENUES
"Average bunch of bourgeoisie"

The Southampton Film Society was inaugurated at a meeting in Price's Cafe, Above Bar (which later became the Classic Cinema) on 14th October 1931. Southampton was one of the pioneers of this movement, being preceded only by London (the first formed 25th October 1925), Glasgow, Edinburgh, Birmingham and Leicester. The film society movement set out to show films, often foreign, which were not generally available and could be loosely titled Arthouse.

Programme for the first season of the Southampton Film Festival.

The first committee included the Mayor as President and Professor A. A. Cock, F. L. Freeman (Chief Education Officer), Reverend R. B. Jolly (St. Mary's) and Harold B. Lankester among its members. Their work was publicised by "Playgoer" (E. A. Mitchell) through his weekly column in the Southern Daily Echo. Their first application for permission to hold performances on a Sunday afternoon was refused by the Buildings and House Drainage Sub-Committee of the Borough Council. Restricted to showing silent films and needing a venue other than a cinema, the society's first performance duly took place on Wednesday 9th December 1931 at the Methodist Central Hall, which was equipped with silent projectors. The main film was Walter Ruttman's *Berlin*, to the accompaniment of a small orchestra.

Finding the Central Hall "too large and not sufficiently central", the Society quickly moved to Avenue Hall where it completed its first season, having purchased its own projectors, with three hundred members. The Avenue Hall in those days was, as the then Secretary J. S. Fairfax-Jones noted, "...little more than a shed with a corrugated iron roof, extremely uncomfortable..."

By the second season the Council had granted permission for the society to hold three performances on Sunday afternoons, so the programme was a mix of sound and silent films. It also included an "International Exhibition of Film Stills and Literature" at Price's Restaurant. Activities were curtailed by the Second World War but the Society was revived in 1946 by, amongst others, Fairfax-Jones, Constance Sewell and the Curator of the Art Gallery, Loraine Conran. Conran, who had spent his war time "dreaming of a small lecture theatre at the Art Gallery, to house a film society", later reflected, at a time when the society had up to 1,000 members, that perhaps "I should have planned for a large extension at the Regent (the venue of the Society) to house the Art Gallery." Latterly his dream has become reality with the lecture theatre in the NorthGuild complex equipped to show film.

The Society used a variety of venues over the years, mainly the Regent in Shirley, whose manager, Ernie Cox, helped select films. Other venues included the Atherley and Classic Cinemas and the Physics Theatre at Southampton University. Special children's matinees were arranged at Christmas, featuring unusual films such as the Russian made *Stone Flower*. Another speciality was midnight matinees featuring the classic silent films of Buster Keaton and Harold Lloyd, accompanied on piano by Arthur Dulay.

It is probably true to say that the society attracted the local intelligentsia or "would-be intelligentsia", a stereotype which Anthony Brode, the then drama and film critic of the Echo, lampooned in the following poem, written under the pen name of 'Rex Moller'

THE DEVOTEES

In corduroys, bow-ties and slacks,
In capes and coats and plastic macs
And garments like potato sacks
The cultured sit enthralled.

(By tram and bus and car they come -
And little beards are worn by some,
And some are rather bald).

Hair may be worn across one eye:
The college scarf may hide the tie,
But brows must everywhere be high
Among the two-and-threes.

(And as they wait to see the show.
They swap an epigram or so
And talk Lejeunalese).

For this is Sunday afternoon:
And experts will be seeing soon
A film to make a critic swoon -
No British picture, this!

(But good, because it's French or Dutch
Hungarian, or something such,
Italian, or Swiss).

Constance Sewell, for the lampooned, replied:

Lucky " Rex Moller", able to report
He overheard some comment of a sort
Weaving across the foyer's jolly noise:
It is not often anyone can learn
Where we dissent from Whitebait or Lejeune,
Or catch us with our beards and corduroys.
(Our men are apt to wear their formal shirts,
Our girls their dolman sleeves and new-
length skirts).

Through records of Debussy as we wait
Not all the things we call to those and these
Relate to cultural activities
"Sequence" or "Documentary 48."
And here are more than all the usual faces
From college, concert and the lecture places.
We do not hope to drop an epigram
As from the film we mass towards the tram.
Indeed we are (and quite content to be)
A pretty average bunch of bourgeoisie.

By the late 1960's the popularity of television was reducing cinema attendances generally and the Film Society movement proved no exception. The Southern Evening Echo of 24th September 1969 noted with "considerable regret that we have to announce the closure of the Southampton Film Society."

More recently, however, its traditions have been revived by the aptly named Phoenix Film Theatre, in association with the University Staff Club, which shows selected films at the Bolderwood Centre, Bassett Crescent East.

Outdoor Cinema Van

Permission was given by the Council for an outdoor cinema van being sited on Kingsland Square in August 1949 to show films (short cine-review type) of British Industry at work and its contribution to the general community.

Cinerama Mobile Theatre

The Cinerama mobile theatre toured England in 1963 and 1965, backed by Cyril and Bernard Mills of Bertram Mills Circus fame, who also supplied the Big Top. The marquee could hold 1,222 seats and was transported on 49 wagons, trailers and caravans. It visited Southampton at a site in West Quay Road on 22nd September 1965.

The first Cinerama film was shown in 1952 and the first full length feature film *How the West Was Won* was shown on this tour.

Mountbatten Theatre, East Park Terrace

From the 1970's films were shown in the large hall of Southampton Institute of Higher Education. It had a balcony and utilised temporary seating on the ground floor. It also was a venue in Southampton's Film Festival. Cinema was ended in April 1990 when the hall was converted into a library.

FILM FESTIVAL
"A decade of success in the cinema"

The credits started rolling on the first Southampton Film Festival in 1986 and soon the fortnight-long event established itself as the South's biggest celebration of cinema. For a decade, screens around the city have enjoyed their busiest two weeks of the year with a programme emphasising variety and drawing on the best in film from all over the world.

Established before the opening of the MGM Multiplex at Ocean Village, one of the most successful multi-screen cinemas in the country, the first two events were held in fondly remembered High Street picture palaces - the Odeon and the ABC. The Gantry Community Arts Centre and the Mountbatten Theatre (now the Southampton Institute Library) were among the first venues for the festival.

Organised and funded by Southampton City Council, the festival relied on sponsorship from enthusiastic private sector partners. Its main aim is to provide a programme which appeals to people from all parts of the community.

As well as regional premieres and previews of the latest hits from Hollywood and the European film industry, community events, workshops and themed mini-seasons were also a regular feature in a packed two weeks of cinematic events. The festival also provided a forum to explore issues including racism, HIV awareness and the portrayal of women in film.

Southampton, over the years, has attracted its fair share of movie celebrities including directors Bryan Forbes, Mike Leigh, Gurinder Chadha, Terry Gilliam and Bill Douglas.

INTERVIEWEES

Dorothy McAllen, Née Barrett. Born 1913, Portswood. Attended Bevois Town School. Dorothy started work at Russells Shoe shop in St. Mary's and then through her Uncle who was Chief Operator at the Atherley Cinema in Shirley, got a job as an Usherette. She worked at the Atherley and the Broadway for approximately five years and then went as a cashier at the Plaza in 1932 when it first opened. She stayed at the Plaza until 1935 when she got married.

Jack Buck. Outside the Atherley Cinema, now a Bingo Hall. 1996. Born 1909. Shirley. Jack's father, William Dalton Buck, built the Atherley cinema in Shirley and the Broadway in Portswood. Jack became manager of the Atherley at twenty one years of age and his brother managed the Broadway. Jack later opened a car salesroom at the top of Hill Lane.

John Cooper. At the Plaza c.1940. Born 1923. Cheshire. The family moved south when John's father, a seaman was transferred with White Star Line. Attended western district school. On leaving school John went to work as a page boy at the Regal cinema in the High Street. Several months later he progressed to the projection room. After six months as fifth projectionist he became fourth projectionist at the Plaza in Northam in 1938. In 1941 John joined the RAF until 1946, returned to the Plaza for a short while and finally went to work in the aircraft industry.
"I enjoy wide screens now and the sound, and of course, no smoke, the smoke was a problem in those days, it's a wonder we all didn't get cancer, you were constantly in thick smoke all the time in the cinema itself... and to go now is sheer pleasure."

Colin Brenton. Outside the former site of the Plaza, now Meridian T.V. Studios. 1996. Born 1928. Swaythling. From 1943 - 1953 excluding National Service Colin worked at the Plaza in Northam, first as a re-wind boy and later as second projectionist. One of his early jobs was to take the newsreels by bus from the Plaza to the Odeon in the High Street.

INTERVIEWEES

Sam Cooper. Born 1925. Shirley. Brother of John he also went to the Regal as a page boy in 1939 and a few months later became the fourth projectionist. During the blitz on Southampton Sam and another fifteen year old were left alone to run the films while outside the town was burning. Sam left the cinema industry in the early 1940's to take up an apprenticeship with Folland Aircraft Co. and spent the rest of his working life in the aircraft industry.

Marjorie Hanley, née Tucker. On the site of the Palladium. 1996. Born 1920. Bedford Place. One of her early memories is visiting the Empire in Commercial Road and seeing Gracie Fields in a stage and film show. Marjorie also remembers visiting the Palladium in Portswood, her favourite cinema where her in-laws went so often that they had their names put on two seats in the back row.

John Fanstone. Outside the site of the Ritz Cinema in Bitterne, now Bitterne Bowl. Born 1923. High Street. John was allowed to leave school just before his fourteenth birthday to get a job at the Ritz in Bitterne which had just opened. One of his first jobs was to cycle to Woolston Cinema with the Newsreels. He went on to become Chief Projectionist/Manager and Relief Manager at other cinemas within the Harry Mears Company. After serving in the navy during the second world war he returned to the Ritz until 1957. John then went to Woolston and became the Company Manager until his retirement.

Eric Martin. Born 1925 St. Deny's. Attended St. Deny's school until 1939 when he left just before his 14th Birthday in 1940 and got a job at the Palladium in Portswood at a salary of five shillings and sixpence a week. Eric progressed to a projectionist and worked at the Savoy, Classic and Forum cinemas with time out for service in the Fleet Air Arm.

DREAM PALACES

Walter G. Olive. On the site of the Kings Cinema, Kingsland Square. 1996. Born 1916. Chapel. Whilst still a schoolboy Walter became a boot repairers runner for a Mr. Hood who repaired footwear for Cleveland's Boot Shop in the High Street. He was paid a shilling a week, he gave sixpence to his mother and saved the rest until he had enough to buy a small hand projector which he used for showing films in his garden shed in Grove Street. During the second world war Walter served with the First Battalion Hampshire Regiment, the first British troops to land in France on D-Day.

Fred Smith. Mayflower Theatre. 1996. Born 1915. Ludgershall. Started as a Junior Projectionist at the Plaza in 1932. He also worked at the Cinenews, Savoy, Forum and during the second world war at the Gaumont. After retirement from the Ordnance Survey he returned to the Gaumont as relief projectionist and stage doorkeeper for fourteen years.

David Meech. Eighteen year old student at Taunton's College. A keen cinema enthusiast, David visits the cinema at least twice a week. "My favourite film is Return of the Jedi... ... I like it when they do special previews because I saw "Die Hard with a Vengeance" which was followed by "Crimson Tide" before they were on general release."

Irene Taylor, née Becheley. On the site of the former Regent Cinema. 1996. Born 1924. Chapel. During the war Irene was evacuated to Wincanton, Somerset where she got a job as a projectionist at the local Plaza, she was 16 years old. On her return to Southampton she worked as the second projectionist at the Regent from 1950 - 1955.
"Mario Lanza was my favourite filmstar and every time I was making the film up we used to inspect it every so often, and when it came to a close up, just a frame of his face, I would cut that out, splice the film again, a frame has got about twelve so it was only one frame out of those twelve that was missing, you can always tell when a film has been cut or spliced because when the sound's going through there's a little bang on the screen, a bang on the sound, and a sort of jump, I kept them for quite some years."

INTERVIEWEES

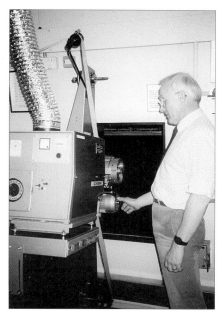

Brian Turner. In the projection room of the Harbour Lights Cinema. Born 1937 in Romford, Essex. He became interested in cinema from an early age and after a variety of jobs entered "the business" as a trainee projectionist at the Southampton Odeon in 1964 where he remained till 1984, by then senior projectionist. After a year as a projectionist for P & O at sea he returned to the Odeon as chief from 1985 until its closure in 1993. Since February 1995 he has been Cinema Operations Manager at Harbour Lights. "There is the Cinema Theatre Association, which I am a member of actually, which is very strong, they are very strong in the cinema buildings, the history of cinema."

Rod Varley. In the Harbour Lights Cinema. Born 1959. Farnham, Surrey. Studied various photography and film studies courses at Manchester Polytechnic, Trent Polytechnic and Derbyshire College of Higher Education. Formerly Head of Film at the National Museum of Photography and Television, responsible for the Pictureville Cinema and Cinerama projects. He is currently Chief Executive of the Southampton Film Company which runs Harbour Lights Cinema.

John Harris. Born 1941. Dover. Came to live in Woolston when he was about three years old. When he left school he got a job as a trainee projectionist at the Regent in Shirley where he stayed until it closed down in 1962. Being a cinema buff, John says he took to the job 'like a duck to water' and spent his evenings off 'going to the cinema'.

Nash Ladher. Outside the Singh Sabha Gurudwara Temple, formerly St. Lukes Church Hall. Born 1950. Nairobi, Kenya. Moved to Southampton in 1966. First became interested in film in the mid 1970's when he was involved in setting up a club showing Indian films in St. Lukes Hall. He was also involved in showing film at the Gantry. Today Nash lives in Newtown and works as a printer.

DREAM PALACES

Leslie Bradfield. Born 1907. Came to live in Bitterne where his father, a master Butcher opened a shop. Attended Bitterne and Taunton schools. When he was eighteen Leslie played the violin for the silent films at the Bitterne Cinema. A keen sportsman Leslie became a professional tennis coach in the 1940's and with his wife set up a very successful tennis school.

Thomas Hiett. With shunt regulator used at the Picture Palace. Born 1929. Hamble. Electrician. Worked with Archie Reade who was an early cinema projectionist at the Empire in French Street. Thomas also worked at the Odeon and Picture House repairing world war two bomb damage.

Pamela Humphrey, née Bowles Born 1936. Freemantle. Her parents ran Strong's Off Licence in Firgrove Road. As a child Pamela was a Junior Member of the Odeon Cinema Club. Pamela now lives in Millbrook and takes a very keen interest in local history.

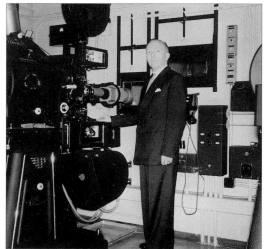

Bert Mayell. At the British Board of Film Censors. Born 1923. Itchen. Started as a re-wind boy at the Rialto in Shirley, then went to the Abbey in Netley in 1938 when it first opened, as a projectionist. During the second world war Bert served with the Eighth (Belfast) Heavy Anti-Aircraft Regiment and later transferred to the Indian Army where he ran a mobile cinema 'The Mobile Jungle Ritz-Odeon'. After the war he became Chief Projectionist at the British Board of Film Censors in London.
"Oh there was only one picturehouse, the Woolston. Woolston pictures plays a large part in my cinema life. I've been into luxury cinemas, I've been in the bug-hutches, I've served in cinemas all over the place but Woolston is a flea-pit, but it's my love."

and Jill Neale, Clare Wilson, Kirpal Vedwan, Harbhajan, Marilyn Michalowicz, Julie Browne and Ken Russell.

Also thanks to all those who have been interviewed for the Oral History Archive since 1983 and whose extracts have been included in this publication.

BIBLIOGRAPHY

Cathedrals of the movies. David Atwell. The Architectural Press Limited

Halliwells Film Guide

Hampshire Magazine

Picture Palace. A Social History of the cinema. Audrey Field. Published by Gentry Books 1974.

Southampton at War 1939 - 1945. L.A. Burgess. Published by Friends of Old Southampton.

Southampton Cinemas. John C. Shepherd Mercia Cinema Society 1994.

Southampton Film Society, One Hundred Programmes 1931 - 1952.

Southern Daily Echo

The Bulletins of the Cinema Theatre Association.

The Picture Palace. Denis Sharp. Printed by Hugh Evelyn. London

What's On, Southampton Pictorial, and other local newspapers are available on microfilm, in the Local Studies section of the Southampton Central Library.

A British Picture. An Autobiography. Ken Russell. Heinman 1989.

Leanord Maltin's Movie and Video Guide. Signet 1995.

Cinema Theatre Association:
This organisation gives its members the opportunity to visit theatres and cinemas nationwide. For details send a self-addressed envelope to William Wren, Flat 30, Cambridge court, Southend-on-Sea, Essex, SS1 1EG.

ACKNOWLEDGEMENTS

Art Asia
Ian Abrahams, Bitterne Local History Society
Brazier and Son Limited, Builders
Padmini Broomfield, Assistant Community Services Librarian
Andy Buchanan, The Gantry
Wally Chalk
Margery Chappell, née Chivers
Mrs Lynda Chantler
Alan Corbishley
Dr. Edwin Course
Carol Curtis
Eddie Dawe
Glen Day
David Friend
Mike Hammond, Southampton Institute of Higher Education
Hampshire Magazine
John Henton
Harbour Lights Cinema Staff
Mr. Illes
Imperial War Museum
A.G.K. Leonard
Paul Lewis, Steve Jarrett and Dick Vidler of the Mayflower Theatre
John Edgar Mann
Tony Martin
Mount Pleasant Media Workshop
Ocean Pictures Cruising Ltd.
Myra Shacklady, Stena Line
Richard Sheaf
Southern Daily Echo
Special Collections Library Staff
Brian Ticehurst
Jill Waterhouse

Oral History Interviewers
Sheila Jemima
Donald Hyslop
Jean Berry
Padmini Broomfield
Tim Caves
Carl Major
Sharon Taffe
Christine Tanner

Southampton City Council Staff
Thanks to our colleagues in different departments for their help:
Dr. Andy Russel, Alastair Arnott, Rachel Wragg, Ingrid Peckham (Heritage Services), Janet Pontin, Mike Williams and Barbara Wilson (Environmental Planning), Mike Douglas, Danny Hillhouse and with special thanks to Wendy Barker and Sandra Barrett for the design and typesetting (Public Relations & Graphics Services), Sue Woolgar, Andrew George, Mark Baverstock and John Masters (Southampton Archive Service) and last but not least, Simon Hardy, Heritage Services Manager for his continued support.